Massaging the Mindset

Massaging the Mindset

An Intelligent Approach to Systemic Change in Education

Felecia Nace

ROWMAN & LITTLEFIELD

Lanham • Boulder • New York • London

Published by Rowman & Littlefield
A wholly owned subsidiary of The Rowman & Littlefield Publishing Group, Inc.
4501 Forbes Boulevard, Suite 200, Lanham, Maryland 20706
www.rowman.com

Unit A, Whitacre Mews, 26-34 Stannary Street, London SE11 4AB

British Library Cataloguing in Publication Information Available

Library of Congress Cataloging-in-Publication Data

Library of Congress Cataloging-in-Publication Data Available

ISBN 978-1-4758-1214-5 (cloth : alk. paper)
ISBN 978-1-4758-1215-2 (pbk. : alk. paper)
ISBN 978-1-4758-1216-9 (electronic)

♾™ The paper used in this publication meets the minimum requirements of American National Standard for Information Sciences Permanence of Paper for Printed Library Materials, ANSI/NISO Z39.48-1992.

Printed in the United States of America

Contents

Acknowledgments

This book is dedicated to Norman. The angels reclaimed one of their own.

Thank you to the following: Pete Tambouro, Ton Duif, Darell Rud, Annamarie Nucci, M.D., and Euan Mackie.

A very special thank you to Opal and Rhonie Wright.

And of course, J. T.

Chapter One

Are Leaders Preparing Teachers for Change?

INTRODUCTION—THE IMPORTANCE OF MASSAGING THE MINDSET

Massaging the mindset involves planting the proper seeds in individuals that will harvest desired results. This book explores ways leaders can prepare the mindsets of those in education to meet the challenges of new concepts and initiatives in the field of education. There are many new initiatives in education that are well-meaning but lack the proper alignment of ethos. That is not to say that everyone in a given system should be in a continuous state of agreement, but mindsets need to be aligned fundamentally for the "good of the cause." It is only then that systemic change can become a possibility.

Too often, due to a lack of staff cohesiveness, there is mere partial implementation of sound effective practices in schools. Administrators agree that staff mindsets play a pivotal role in successful implementation. Yet, not all know how to effectively massage the mindset. Administrators are aware that collective thinking can

1

move changes forward in a quick and efficient manner. Therefore, school systems need to directly and assertively address systemic change issues.

System-wide cultivation of initiatives is essential to improving school outcomes. This requires that systemic thinking be a part of a school's DNA. If this level of cohesive thinking is not prevalent, then there exists a need for internal professional learning that directly addresses mindset issues in the workplace.

In cases where change is slow to take shape or stagnant, leaders struggle with keeping their own morale intact. Moving initiatives forward presents a challenge for many leaders. It is for this reason that effective administrators opt for a systemic methodology as a roadmap to full implementation. When school issues arise or new initiatives are introduced, everyone connected to that school is affected. In some instances, change occurs quickly but lacks quality. Over the years, many federal and state education specialists have shared in the frustration of district administrators, school administrators, teachers, as well as parents, as it relates to effective, expedient change.

Since meeting school goals requires a unified effort, here are some pertinent questions toward that end: Are school districts forming the necessary alliances? Do educational leaders understand how the mind processes change? Do administrators teach staff and other stakeholders how effective change takes shape? These questions speak directly to building capacity. A smart goal would be to mobilize staff to think collectively on a fundamental level. Then, schools can construct strategic partnerships both internally and externally that will have a real impact on school climate, instruction, and leadership.

Oftentimes, when school and district administrators are engaged in conversations regarding building capacity among staff, it is associated with improving instruction. Before schools can accomplish any specific teaching and learning goals, staff members need to know what effective change looks like. Many leaders are aware that systemic change is by far the best means of reaching goals because it takes into account everyone and every aspect of a desired change. However, leaders should not gamble and assume that staff members are knowledgeable about the dynamics of how to participate in collective transitions.

The study of systemic change is necessary in every school, as it is at the root of every shared vision. Consequently, administrators need to understand a staff's perceptions of change so that the leader can gauge where each individual falls on the change continuum. Then leaders can meet staff members where they are as they work to engage staff in the educational transitions.

There is also a need for school administrators to teach staff how to engage family and community members. Instructional leaders know that children don't fail themselves. The same holds true for teachers. Teachers who lack the proper tools to stay abreast of current trends are not totally to blame. Many teachers' downfalls can be traced back to leadership.

An educational leader's focus would be well spent developing change skillsets in those they lead. Instructional leaders are charged with coaching staff through challenges in the change process, sharing viable resources that focus on systemic change, and providing strategies that facilitate progressiveness. Change, in itself, is a topic to be studied by all staff members. At the center of the study of change is the study of "self"—all that make up the personality.

Only then can schools get to the root of change issues and establish the right foundation to move initiatives forward.

Constructive Psychology and Change

If you want to know how effectively school administrators are carrying out their duties, you might begin by surveying parents and school staff. However, if you desire to know how schools can create effective changes, consult a psychiatrist. This book was designed based on the premise that there is a psychological aspect to change that is often bypassed, but is a major factor in transforming schools. The conversation surrounding change in U.S. school systems would not be complete without the infusion of the study of psychology.

Over the past century, psychologists have been at the center of change in education. Notably, Jean Piaget, Madeline Hunter, and Howard Gardner have all made major progressive contributions to teaching and learning shifts. Much of change has to do with a shift in the mindset of people. Why then, do some educational leaders hesitate to turn to psychology when they desire to implement major changes?

When an educational leader sets out to create a substantive change in a school district, it is useful to know the basic characteristics of people who may be resistant to change. After all, parents, teachers, and educational leaders are all driven by their respective psyches. Therefore, a refresher course on basic human emotion and response makes for good background knowledge when leaders are faced with mindsets that oppose positive change. Before leaders can massage the mindsets of those around them, they must first anticipate and be prepared to address myriad change issues that may arise.

Psychology has relevance in the world of education, especially as it relates to educational transformations. Over the years, psychiatrists have shed light on how the mindset works. For example, in 1923, Sigmund Freud introduced to the world some fundamentals of human behavior in the form of the id, the ego, and the superego. Many psychologists continue to build on those fundamental theories. Psychologists understand that change comes about by first understanding and acknowledging basic human behavior.

Collective Movement

A skillful leader knows how to bring forth change. Besides studying basic human behavior, systems thinking is another important topic for school administrators to study before attempting to implement changes. It is a way of thinking that is inclusive of all parties and is all encompassing of concepts and strategies across the curriculum.

For example, in getting staff to think systemically, a visual aspect to growth and development can connect staff and should not be overlooked. Advertisers stimulate the onlooker all the time through sound and visual cues. Throughout a given office building, offices in the business sector often display plenty of graphs and charts that outline goals, successes, and challenges. These aids are often highly visible.

Graphs and charts represent the journey of an organization. They engender a teamwork approach among staff. In a sense, using them is a way of keeping score—measuring the results of collective hard work. Staff members can track the results of their methodologies, clearly identifying stagnant periods, progression, and decline.

However, schools rarely openly display such charts and graphs. After professional learning has taken place, staff members can benefit from seeing vivid reminders of their target goals strategically exhibited throughout a school building. Charts and graphs that are representative of school goals and progress could line school hallways, administrators' offices, and teachers' lounges and can serve as effective "mental massagers" for those practices school and district leaders desire to fully implement. Charts and graphs that demonstrate progress should also be shared electronically with staff on a consistent basis.

Besides the obvious visual cues, many factors affect how human beings will respond to change. Ingraining messages throughout the workday, however subtle or overt, is a good start. However, a leader must probe deeper and take into account the qualities that every person embodies. This begins by looking at the essence of each staff member.

Mind, Body, Spirit

The mind, body, and spirit alignment is rarely considered when school districts attempt to change the status quo. With tightly packed schedules, bell systems that sound routinely throughout the day, and the daily bustle of staff and students, one rarely has time to reflect on the three important factors that need consistent nurturing—the mind, body, and spirit of all shareholders within a system. The alignment of these three elements provides support for effective transformations to take shape.

Understanding behavior is a chief part of leadership. Too often, the layered work that needs to be done in leadership roles is dismissed as unnecessary, when in fact, the void of studying the mind and mindsets of people often leads to cyclical problems and continued breakdowns in the workplace. Frequently, disconnects that occur between school leaders and other shareholders in education are primarily based on misperceptions.

From a psychological perspective, instructional leaders should possess the ability to view staff members as individuals with individual lives and backgrounds who are coming together for a common cause. Leaders cannot afford to discount the backstories of staff. Not only are staff members bringing with them countless harvested experiences, but leaders must also consider each mind, body, and spiritual experience separately in individuals and how those experiences collectively affect the whole person. Leaders have the advantage of observing how unique background experiences impact the whole group, and can tactically use that data.

The staff members whom school administrators have hired and see before them each day are complex individuals—not just Mr. Q who is resistant to change, or Mrs. J, the overachiever. They weren't born that way. It is unacceptable for leaders to say that they simply don't have time to examine individual mindsets, because change cannot occur without first understanding the three main elements that make up human beings. When leaders treat people as though they have been manufactured on an assembly line, the result is overwhelmingly negative.

What relevance do mind, body, and spirit have in school settings? If administrators respect the attributes that staff, students, families, and communities bring to the educational experience, then perhaps teachers can gain a deeper understanding of differentiation—taking into account the mind, body, and spirit of students as they tailor learning. Let's further examine each component in relation to the school environment.

Mind. It's no secret that the mind is an *intricate* instrument. The background experiences of a person such as environment, schooling, family life, level of intellectual interactions, among other factors, determine how one problem-solves, processes information, and reacts to situations. In addition, issues in one's personal life can add stress and impede performance. Accordingly, if a person is not experiencing an abundance of stress outside of the workplace, this can enhance one's clarity so the individual is better able to accomplish the goals at-hand. Varied factors in one's life can determine how a person addresses change.

Body. Health and nutrition must be considered. Often, adult nutrition is overlooked in a school environment. As it concerns nutrition and overall wellness, educators tend to place emphasis on children's diets and physical fitness. In recent years, schools have focused careful attention on students' nutritional intake as it directly correlates to their academic performance. It is commonly known that if a person does not receive the proper nutrition, has poor health, and lacks proper rest, he/she will not function optimally. Likewise, promoting healthy lifestyles among school staff can improve staff members' quality of life and can determine their level of energy at work.

Spirit. The spirit is not tangible. It is that thing that one cannot touch but is certainly sensed. In many ways, the spirit of individuals is directly linked to school culture and climate. It is part of the tone, energy, and pulse of a school that people recognize when they walk through a school building. When serious attention is paid to enriching the culture and climate of a school, academic outcomes have been known to improve.

Simply taking interest in the mind, body, and spirit can raise the level of consciousness about systemic change beginning with the human system. The teaching profession needs educators who arrive at school each day ready to meet the challenges that education entails. Teaching is not a simple job, nor is it meant to be. It is an art. This requires teachers and other staff members to be "complete."

Before one can truly think systemically and commit to a systemic working environment, that person must first arrive at work "whole." Otherwise, staff members who may desire to contribute to systemic changes can be encumbered by a slew of outside influences that hinder active participation. As much as possible, attention must be paid to the wellness of staff, as this is a significant part of preparing teachers for transitions. In order to effectively address issues that concern employees, administrators must build trusting relationships with staff. This step helps develop a keen understanding of staff culture, which is essential to planning wellness sessions for staff.

Tips for Promoting Wellness in the Workplace:

1. Collaborate with health-care professionals in the school district and community to select relevant materials to distribute to staff on a regular basis. This may include free reliable websites that promote healthy habits.

2. Invite motivational speakers to kick off the school year, or to reenergize staff mindsets midyear. As the school leader, create your own motivational activities to begin staff meetings, especially when you sense that morale is low.

3. School leaders can seek out health-care professionals at local hospitals who are willing to provide workshops to staff on the topic of stress. Subtopics may include how to detect when stress levels are high and stress management tips. Some psychology intern programs require interns to conduct action research, which includes providing free workshops in the community.

4. Share with staff those things you have altered in your lifestyle to offset stress and to enjoy a healthier existence. If the leader

serves as a living example, this may encourage staff members to rethink their own unhealthy habits.

SYSTEMS THINKING AND EDUCATIONAL SYSTEMS

Systems thinking entails thinking about the connectivity of subsystems (parts) to the whole system. For example, a school system fosters K–12 education, but within that system there exist subsystems such as individual grade levels, specialized classes, instructional staff, noninstructional staff, parents, and administrators. Systems thinking forces these subsystems to reflect on individual and group contributions—how each one impacts the other as well as the whole system—and highlights the impact that subsystems collectively have on end goals.

Systemic thinking not only entails taking into account and examining all the parts that make up a whole. It is also necessary to identify the strengths and weaknesses that exist within a system. It seeks to understand how a system functions. For instance, a systems-thinking framework is designed to acknowledge outside influences and discover how a system, such as a school system, interacts or overlaps with other systems in society.

Often, educators are not exposed to a systems thinking course in colleges and universities until they enter a leadership program, studying theorists like Fritjof Capra. Until this opportunity presents itself to an educator, systems thinking and systemic change can hold abstract meanings for that individual. If they lack background knowledge on the topic, leaders cannot expect that staff will grasp the true definition of collective change.

There are leaders who look back and examine major events from their early years in education. Many memorable moments required a systems-thinking skillset, and it has led many administrators to question why they had not been exposed to systems thinking prior to attending graduate school. They realize that as young teachers or even as student-teachers, had they possessed the knowledge to effectively collaborate with shareholders, they could have saved valuable time and frustration.

School and district administrators know all too well how the study of systems thinking can sharpen one's looking glass. Elements of systemic thinking can be woven into professional learning sessions. Leaders can equip teachers with the knowledge they need to circumvent comfort zones that act as traps and inevitably are detrimental to the teaching and learning process. Therefore, the study of effective change is a precursor to the implementation of any instructional practices.

Many elements of systems thinking are invaluable when interfacing with students, parents, administrators, community members, and colleagues—all vital components of the educational system. An ill-equipped teacher cannot appreciate the connectivity that is shared among these seemingly individual groups.

Veteran administrators as well as veteran teachers can recall what it was like entering into the profession. Many administrators began their careers as wide-eyed and hopeful teachers, only to encounter negative comments in teachers' lounges made by veteran teachers complaining about the constant changes in education, poor student behavior, and miscommunication between teachers and parents, unaware that they themselves were the change agents. Teachers entering into the field of education need to be change-ready.

The most important lesson that educators can internalize is that change in any system is constant and a system is only as strong as the forces that propel it. A poignant lesson that any leader can derive from studying systems thinking is that in order to make effective changes, every element involved in a given system must understand, whether by instinct or learned behavior, the common goals and the essential role that each change agent will play. All components in a given system are continually affecting change.

Whether a component provides positive input, negative input, or chooses to remain neutral, that component contributes something to the function of a system and is part of the change process, irrespective of the individual's awareness of his/her role. As it stands, very few school systems possess a common definition of *systems thinking* or *systemic change*. Developing a common understanding of systems thinking can provide a starting point for moving ideas forward in our intricate educational systems.

With increasing awareness of systems thinking, educational leaders in varied capacities are being challenged to view systemic change as a behavior that can be learned and a skill to be honed. If leaders approach change from this perspective, then leaders can provide targeted learning opportunities for student-teachers, new teachers, and veteran teachers to fully grasp the concepts of systemic change and all that it entails. It is through the study of systems thinking that leaders become discerning about how to construct an engrained, cooperative working environment.

Once an educator has been exposed to systems thinking, teaching and learning experiences are enhanced and working relationships within school districts become more meaningful. As school culture and other factors change, it is likely that end goals will change as well. Subsequently, staff will need to be flexible and amenable to new ideas.

Shifting one's perception of change alters the approach one decides to take toward implementing practices. A good measure of progressive leadership will be how leaders approach the task of creating, not sustainable changes, as educators have often heard in the past, but instead, sustainable lifelong learners in themselves, teachers, noninstructional staff, parents, and students. If administrators accomplish this goal in a given school system, then they create a staff that is consistently fluid.

Fostering Systemic Mindsets

Educators can become complacent as any worker might. However, with so much at stake, an educator who works in any capacity cannot afford to view a position as just a job. Instead, all educators, whether a teacher's assistant or superintendent, are key components of a system that affects other systems that critically depend on the quality of a school's input and output.

Since leaders understand the important role education plays in society, why then do the theories of systems thinking and systemic change remain elusive concepts for staff, parents, and community members? There is much conversation about promoting collective movement in school districts, but the development of such skills is sorely lacking. In short, skill development must equal the desire to change resistant behavior and fragmented approaches.

For many, in the United States, systemic change is learned behavior, largely due to an American upbringing wherein Western culture is adept at nurturing individualism. For example, in the Japanese culture, it is commonly known that the word "I" is nonexistent in the Japanese vocabulary. That single omission from the language speaks volumes about how deeply collective thinking is embedded in Japanese daily lives. Imagine a world without the word "I."

Systems thinking is evident in every aspect of life in Japan, from the way people casually share food from their plates when entertaining in large groups, to the way the Japanese board the subways in Tokyo. Anyone who has ever visited Tokyo can tell you that boarding subways in Tokyo is a very different experience from boarding subways in New York, Washington, D.C., or Chicago. In the United States, it can be every man for himself. That's not to say that would-be riders take leave of their senses, or that U.S. commuters are void of common courtesies. However, in contrast, commuters on Tokyo subway platforms take a different approach. For example, it is customary to form a line before boarding a subway car. If you ask a Japanese native why they form a line, one might simply say, "It's the safest way to board the train." Thinking about the system as a whole is always top of mind for the Japanese. These are just a few examples of holistic thinking in a series of lessons that one could learn by studying Eastern culture.

Certainly, not all the answers to educational issues lie in systems thinking, but there are basic aspects of cohesive thinking that can be learned, taught, and cultivated in Western culture if leaders desire change to take shape quickly in educational systems. Recently, there has been much discussion about transformational leadership in education. However, while many educational leaders promote "out of the box" thinking, the reality remains that countless schools are still entrenched in very traditional roots.

Change Issues and Professional Growth

School leaders have confessed that creating a systemic change is their primary challenge. Yet, if asked to produce records of professional learning (PL) sessions that were provided to staff during the school year, rarely can one find evidence that schools provided systems thinking workshops, systems change workshops, or even workshops regarding the change process. There is usually little to no professional development provided to staff regarding change as a primary topic.

The typical professional learning session listed in a school principal's PL documentation will likely focus on specific changes the school desires to implement in respective subject areas. Full implementation is challenging for many schools, irrespective of how celebrated or low the summative test scores, because even the most prominent schools strive to elevate standards and establish new goals. Leaders must broaden their scope of implementation.

There are leaders who assume that if they provide a particular workshop around a specific subject area, staff will naturally make a transition. Even if the change makes perfect sense and it is presented in a way that is engaging, the actual change process still needs to be addressed separately and then woven into the fabric of specific desired changes in order for a real transformation to occur.

Staying mindful that humans are creatures of habit, change should be approached with patience, guidance, and understanding. It is incumbent upon educational leaders to ensure that the learning environment for staff is conducive to open discussions about change, such as how change brings forth exciting challenges and growth, how change can be demanding of one's time, and how painful it can be for people to change—letting go of comfort zones. In order for change to develop, honest conversations need to occur. The school environment should be open to alternative ways to share fears and implement changes.

Topics surrounding change have presented multiple challenges for school leaders. A well-respected New Jersey psychologist, Dr. Annamarie Nucci, was asked: Why do people cling to comfort zones so fervently, even when individuals know that a desired change may enhance their career, personal life, or relationships? She replied:

- What we call a *comfort zone* is a psychological space that holds activities and behaviors that minimize stress and risk. Comfort zone activities are different for every individual, but all provide a haven of minimal stress and anxiety. It is because of this that they are relinquished with reluctance and great difficulty.
- When we are in our comfort zone, we can lay back and "take it easy," and so to speak not do very much. Unfortunately, psychological studies have shown that staying in a "comfort zone" leads to losing ambition and drive, since there are no expectations (of self) that have to be met.
- There are psychological studies that have shown that for optimal performance, we need a state of mild anxiety. This has been called *optimal anxiety*, or *productive discomfort*, by psychologists. We know through these studies that "optimal anxiety" is that place where mental productivity and performance reach their peak. The reason for this is that once one moves out of the comfort zone and moves to a state of optimal anxiety, or productive discomfort, there are deadlines and expectations that have to be met, and this leads to increased productivity.

Oftentimes, people do not understand their own behavior and so they remain stagnant. In Dr. Nucci's explanation of why people resist change, there are opportunities for leaders to utilize this information to stimulate self-awareness in employees and lead discussions about something that many people can relate to—productive discomfort. There are times when all of us have experienced a little "nervous tension," but that tension has often led us to deliver a moving speech or score slightly higher on a test, or has prompted us to go the extra mile on the job.

All leaders have experienced anxiety when faced with a new situation but have rarely given that nervous tension credit for helping enhance performance. This is a great point for leaders to explore with staff. The last thing anyone wants to feel when others are depending on them is nervousness, no matter how slight. It can be an unpleasant experience, but in retrospect, it has often been the "tailwind" that many individuals needed to successfully carry out a task.

If leaders can help staff process their fears and frustrations, then perhaps staff can embrace fear, viewing it as a useful resource rather than a deterrent. This can help give purpose to the anxiety that many people encounter when faced with the prospect of change. Instructional leaders can guide staff in understanding the necessity for a little discomfort and can then collectively confront the trepidation that often impedes forward movement. In short, behaviors that block change can be openly examined and inverted to facilitate the goal of full implementation.

Given the urgency for change in American school systems, there are benefits to rethinking the timeline for exposing educators to systems thinking coursework and a conceptual framework for change. As background research for this book, a cross section of education preparation programs in 200 colleges and universities across the United States were reviewed, and it was discovered that none of these institutions have systems thinking courses as part of the school's teacher preparation programs. This seems ironic, since it is commonly known that working collectively, transitioning, and forming strategic alliances are to be expected throughout an educator's career. However, some of these institutions embed action research projects, which can be beneficial in developing systemic thinking, into their student-teaching models.

Mediocre and failing conditions of many large educational systems across the United States prompt relevant reflective questions regarding the effectiveness of the action research projects that universities offer. Do student-teachers walk away from these action research projects with a comprehensive understanding of systems thinking? Do student-teachers apply relevant information from systems thinking and systemic change theorists to their projects? Do these action research projects have a real impact on the students' teaching careers far beyond the student-teaching experience?

Judging by recent Program for International Student Assessment (PISA) scores and the drop in ranking the United States in the areas of math and science, as well as the projection made by the Center on Education and the Workforce that by 2018 America will need 22 million new workers and will be short by 3 million with college degrees, there is an urgency for leaders to reconsider how change is addressed in the education field. This target is not impossible. However, proper preparation for change can only materialize with swift strategic changes in how educational leaders approach professional learning. The field requires educators who cannot only create change in schools, but who can also sustain a change momentum.

As stated earlier, most educators will be exposed to systems thinking at colleges and universities, but only after they are on administrative tracks. However, these eager administrators return to school districts with their newfound knowledge only to encounter instructional staff members who have difficulty connecting to the idea of systems thinking and systemic change. If the education field can align teachers' and school administrators' knowledge base regarding systems thinking, there can exist an equal playing field so that school administrators and teachers speak a common language about change. Only then can the quality of education improve at a rapid pace.

Supporting Teacher Development

Experience teaches us that too much of a good thing can be detrimental. There can be an overabundance of cohesive thinking wherein one loses creative thought, or one can focus too much on individualism, which contributes to slow collective change. Somewhere there is a balance wherein the two can coexist, complementing one another and creating a breeding ground for innovative transitions. An idea is only as good as the ability to move it forward. That stated, great ideas abound in the field of education, but do school staff members have the capacity to move effective practices forward? This is a key question for leaders. Educational leaders who strive to make the concept of change fluid in their respective school system should consider the following:

1. Do new teachers, student-teachers, veteran teachers, and *all* staff members have a working knowledge of systems thinking and systemic change? Educators need a format for how change will take shape. That includes providing staff with clear definitions, clear direction, and clear goals.

2. Have I properly outlined the benefits of systemic change for those I am preparing for change? It is important that leaders have an answer to the following question: What's in it for me? Anytime any of us have been asked to participate in a transition, we naturally want to know how it will enhance our productivity. It is a fair question and one that school leaders should anticipate from staff.

3. Have I made appropriate systems-thinking materials available to those whom I wish to engage in the change process? Having a professional development library (PDL) in each school is a key component to providing ongoing professional development opportunities to staff and school leaders. Particularly if change is an issue, school leaders will want to ensure that there is a wealth of materials housed in the PDL regarding systemic change (see chapter 3 of this book for examples of relevant theorists).

4. Do I interfere with the change process? This is a great reflective question that leaders should ask themselves, and it is a difficult one because it is always so much easier to blame someone else in a system when desired change is not apparent. This question keeps leaders reflective, alert, and honest about their own contributions to educational processes.

5. Do the people who I want to engage in a systemic change understand that change is constant in any educational setting? Particularly, teaching staff members need to understand and embrace the fact that change is a staple in any teaching and learning environment. This message has to be embedded in professional development. The sooner educators internalize this concept, the more likely they will readily adapt to changes.

Redefining Sustainability

In education, it is difficult to engage in a conversation that does not revolve around sustainability, but leaders must be careful about the context in which this term is used. Educational leaders do not want staff members to believe that they will someday arrive at a comfortable place where change will cease. The only "comfortable place" for an educator is to know that research is constant in our field and to expect that methodologies will change. Many transitions occur because the education profession impacts every other field of study, and our work is greatly influenced by societal shifts such as the job market, higher education, technology, and many other outside influences. Therefore, changes on all scales are inevitable.

There are some elements of change that instructional leaders can and should attempt to sustain, such as increased parent participation, steady increase in test scores, and a safe learning environment. Even the dynamics of these factors steadily shift, and educators will need to adapt. Sustaining staff mindsets may prove to be the most feasible goal when administrators talk about sustainability in school systems. "Massaging the mindset" to prepare teachers for continual change in our ever-evolving field can be difficult, but it is a feasible objective.

Dealing with the complexities of the mindset is challenging for many leaders and is a likely reason why some leaders prefer to simply provide professional learning around topics other than systems thinking and systemic change. However, the mindsets of those whom administrators lead can no longer remain off-limits. While no one likes to wake a sleeping giant, there is a need to address the problem of countless funds being spent by school districts in this country on professional learning without evidence of full implementation of effective strategies. It's time to confront the primary obstacle—the psyche.

TEACHERS AS LIFELONG LEARNERS

Only a lifelong learner can truly grasp the concept of the necessity to stay abreast of current trends. So, how do leaders steer staff to a point of continual, systemic thinking? Needless to say, there is no absolute answer to this question. However, it begins by preparing student-teachers, new teachers, and veteran teachers to remain viable in the field of education by fostering lifelong learning skills that will help teachers navigate the many changes in the teaching profession. That lifelong learning preparation should include topics that focus on systems thinking. Teachers, who are already in the field, must be taught, nurtured, and led by example.

When it comes to change, leaders can assume too much about individuals. For example, some leaders believe that professional development regarding the change process is unnecessary because change is a natural part of human development. What leaders may not take into account is the fact that, although people's lives are constantly changing, change can be uncomfortable for many individuals, as countless changes are thrust upon human beings throughout the course of their lives—death, divorce, economic downturns, layoffs, or any other unforeseen roadblocks. So, we can agree that although people continually change, it is sometimes due to elements outside of their control. Therefore, transformations are not always carried out in the most effective manner, as it can be reactionary rather than well planned. In addition, depending on the types of changes people have had to make in their lives, change can carry with it a negative connotation. Given these variances in how people experience change, training instructional staff on how to maximize changes and leverage various elements of change is worth exploring.

The No Child Left Behind Act of 2001 (NCLB) attempted to define a "quality teacher" and ensure that teachers were exposed to a steady stream of professional development. As a result, many states adopted standards outlining the amount of professional development hours teachers should undergo. For example, presently, a teacher in the state of New Jersey is required to earn 100 professional development hours per a five-year period in order to maintain teaching certification. Is this an incentive for lifelong learning, or do teachers adhere to this requirement simply to maintain their employment status? As we know, lifelong learning is an internal drive that many people develop to quench their intellectual curiosity, to increase their knowledge base, and to stay abreast of trends relevant to their professions and personal lives.

For many of us, lifelong learning begins with an external trigger, and then because of personal increased interest, an impetus develops that fosters independent learning. Required professional development hours might lead to lifelong learning habits, but are administrators and policy makers tracking the number of teachers who seek professional development opportunities beyond the required professional development hours in respective states? Those numbers could reveal how effective the mandates are for promoting lifelong learning in the lives of teachers. Effectually, educational leaders desire a system that encompasses continuity in learning. If a culture of continual learning for staff is not already embedded in the organizational structure, then the educational leader is charged with igniting the flame.

Here are five tips for promoting continuous learning among staff members in school systems:

1. Be an active instructional leader. By demonstrating lessons a few times a year or by providing professional development sessions directly to your staff, you break down both real and perceived barriers, gain the trust of staff members, and demonstrate that you are willing to work side by side with staff to implement changes. Your enthusiasm for researching, contin-

ually learning, and sharing knowledge will establish a standard for lifelong learning among staff.

2. Keep your professional development library current and accessible to all staff members, both instructional and noninstructional. You will generate an atmosphere of system-wide internal ongoing professional development.

3. Create a safe haven for teachers, new and veteran, so they can openly admit to errors and learn from their mistakes. Teachers do not have the luxury that most professionals in other professions enjoy—being wrong. Educators' mistakes are often magnified by parents, students, community members, and family members largely due to a myth that educators possess endless pools of knowledge. However, those of us in the field of education know how erroneous that myth is as we consistently mask our own mistakes to avoid public ridicule. Teachers, like anyone else, desire a place that is comfortable to hold honest discussions about trials and errors. These conversations are necessary for growth.

4. Periodically, educational leaders should massage the mindsets of those they lead by discussing change in positive terms. For example, you can identify a staff member who has made an effective transformation. Ask the individual to briefly talk about the change process attached to their transition and the benefits associated with making the change. This can occur in monthly meetings. Simply stated, create opportunities for change to be viewed as positive.

5. Most educational leaders will facilitate instructional staff in setting learning goals at the end of each school year in preparation for the next school year. Be mindful to benchmark these learning goals and find opportunities to revisit them during

the new school year, perhaps during evaluation conferences and one-to-one benchmark meetings. As much as possible, allow the teacher to lead the discussion regarding follow-through on the agreed-upon learning goals.

Facilitating Transitions

One of the most challenging systemic changes that school districts have faced in the last decade has been transitioning from traditional teaching styles to a more student-focused approach to teaching and learning. To confront problematic transitions, leaders must examine the mindsets of those who teach. Teachers are first and foremost human beings with strengths and frailties. What really lies behind the resistance of some teachers to relinquish center stage to students?

For some, the resistance to transitions can be attributed to inadequate professional learning. This directly impacts teachers' comfort levels as it relates to their ability to change. Others become accustomed to teaching using a particular teaching style and simply do not know how to change; they need guidance. Whatever the reason, there are human factors to consider, respect, and address.

Getting educators to embrace continual change lays a foundation for transformational leadership. Administrators should not expect that staff will change blindly without question, and a good administrator remains conscious of that fact, especially when attempting to secure buy-in from staff regarding proposed transitions. Good leaders welcome questions and input regarding change. In fact, a strong leader will present to staff research that supports why a change is necessary.

Even after presenting supporting research and data to staff, which is a great strategy when introducing a change, still a leader cannot expect complete buy-in as there will likely exist opposing

research and opposing expert viewpoints that are worth considering. Leaders should find out what those opposing views are before-
hand, and be prepared to further support their claims. That would
be a prudent approach.

Remaining open to suggestions and maintaining ongoing dialogue with staff about changes creates an environment conducive
to systemic movement. Empathizing with staff and making a real
attempt to understand how someone can fall prey to habitual behavior provide administrators a window to connect with individuals on
a human level and differentiate learning for staff members. This
allows each person to experience a personal level of success as they
collectively move toward common goals. More understanding of
behavior and less assumption will save leaders time.

Empathizing with staff requires thinking as one's staff might
think. For example, when attempting to change traditional teaching
styles, remember that there are teachers who enjoy a captive audience of students and who may find it difficult to surrender the kind
of undivided attention that students can provide in a classroom.
Also, many teachers themselves learned in classrooms through a
lecture format, so that methodology may seem like an ideal strategy
to implement in their own classrooms. Understanding why a behavior is prevalent can help an administrator determine the best approach for changing a circumstance.

Layering Reflective Practice

Well-trained student-teachers, new teachers, and veteran teachers
understand that change cannot occur without the presence of reflective behavior. Reflection as part of the daily routine in teaching and
learning is also learned behavior for many. As Bloom's Taxonomy
teaches, learning through discovery can spark a continuous learning

cycle. This can lead the learner down a road of consistent, analytical reasoning. It is for this reason that educational leaders must facilitate the process of reflection and coach teachers to a point of realization.

It is not enough to provide professional development that focuses on topics such as incorporating technology into learning, differentiation of instruction, flipped classrooms, and student-focused learning. The real challenge is persuading teachers to reflect on their own behavior. Many school and district leaders have had opportunities to peer through various lenses, and many recognize the absence of reflection regarding aspects of teaching and learning, and how the absence of this piece derails progress in schools. Here are a few suggestions for prompting teachers to self-reflect:

1. Lesson plans—A lesson plan can be an extremely valuable medium. It can be a source of consistent communication between administrators and teachers. In my observations, the lesson plan is generally underrated as a conduit for professional growth. Instead of educational leaders reviewing plans and writing generic comments, think about keeping an open line of communication by responding using reflective questions. Instead of making blanket statements like, "You need to demonstrate more differentiation of instruction in your lessons." Consider asking, "Keeping students' individual learning styles in mind, what are some other ways you can present this lesson so that it is effective to all students?" Another valuable question to ask might be, "What are some ways you can incorporate flexible grouping?"

These types of questions, inserted into the plan book as feedback, lead teachers to reflect on chosen methodologies and draw their own conclusions as to how to proceed, especially if the questions relate to professional development topics that the district has already covered. The critical piece for the administrator is to allow time for teachers to reflect and ensure follow-up via e-mail exchanges or a face-to-face meeting. This open line of communication will save administrators time and reduce frustration long-term.

2. Scenario: Bill is consistently sent to the office for behavioral issues in the classroom. It is evident that teacher-centered instruction is the norm in the classes in which he experiences persistent conflicts. It is obvious that changes need to be made by both the student and his teachers if he is going to experience greater levels of success. During a face-to-face conference with teachers, ask teachers to reflect on their daily teaching strategies. This can be done discretely in one-to-one sessions with each teacher.

You will need to have the teacher's plan book available to support the accuracy of teacher reflections. A poignant question to ask would be, "What teaching strategies can you adopt to meet the needs of Bill?" This type of question forces teachers to reflect on their own culpability, view Bill as an individual learner, and reflect on the possible connection between Bill's behavior and present teaching strategies. Allow teachers time to reflect and create an action plan, and then request a follow-up meeting to discuss options.

3. Common planning time is a good time to require that teachers reflect on practices. For example, this could be a five-minute exercise in which one teacher per session reflects on a lesson in conjunction with student behavior—discuss strategies, pros and cons, and ways to make lessons more inclusive. This gives teachers the opportunity to share ideas and ask for peer advice and assistance, and incorporates the practice of reflection into planning.

The old adage, "It's not how you start but how you finish that counts," is probably not the best advice for new administrators. For new school administrators much of your success hinges on how you begin your career. Creating a culture of reflection pays a hefty dividend. When teachers begin to think about their own thinking and how their actions impact a given school system, then school administrators are relieved from what could conceivably be a long relationship of hand-holding.

NOTE

For more information about creating a professional development library in K–12 schools, please visit the National Association of Elementary School Principal's webpage to view the article "Building a Professional Development Library": http://www.naesp.org/principal-janfeb-2013-teacher-staff-development/building-professional-development-library.

Chapter Two

Confronting Obstacles in Schools

OUTSIDE THE BOX: HOW TO GET THERE

Two obstacles that many schools face are improving creative thinking and critical-thinking skills school-wide. Massaging the mindset requires an environment that is conducive to both creative and critical thinking. One of the most notable phrases that has reverberated around the globe both in business and in education has been "outside the box."

Many significant changes in education originated because of divergent thinking. So, what does thinking outside the box entail? It begins with a place in which learners are comfortable exploring ideas.

Oftentimes, that comfort zone is created in a classroom setting. It starts with the learner making simple connections, exploring options with classmates as well as the instructor. Eventually the learner feels comfortable enough to take risks deviating from the norm.

It is difficult, if not impossible, for students to think outside the box without first making basic connections that are often reflective of their environment—home life, neighborhood, culture, and background experiences. However, these connections can easily be overlooked during the teaching and learning process. Therefore, if a school administrator or teacher who grew up in the suburbs becomes gainfully employed in an inner-city school district, for instance, some profound reflection is in order on the part of these individuals. This is the crossroad wherein the "tale of two cities" meet.

A true story: A school leader sat in the back of a fourth-grade classroom and observed a travesty. By the time he had entered into the classroom, one particular reading group had already finished reading a story independently and had begun reviewing the story details with the teacher. The teacher proceeded to ask a question, "What clues in the story gave you an indication that the main character was about to run away?" She began selecting students to answer the question, and although the observer could not recall all the students' responses, there was one that stood out.

One student responded, "I knew he was going to run because he turned his hat backward." The girl who had given this response was described as wearing a bulky sweater and keeping her eyes lowered for most of the lesson, but for this question she sat up a little straighter and thought that she might contribute something insightful. Well, her response was soon dismissed by the teacher with a retort, "No, that's not it." The teacher then went on to choose another student.

Following the lesson, the educational leader did not allow the student to exit the classroom without congratulating her on her response. The school leader then asked her a concise question, "Can you explain your answer?" She did.

The student explained that she had witnessed the boys in her neighborhood turning their hats backward before they took off running. The principal then followed up with a probing question,

"Why do you think they did that?" Her response was. "I believe they did it so that their hats wouldn't fly off." This situation defined what Hilda Taba attempted to impart to educational leaders decades ago in her many writings about the importance of developing teachers' questioning techniques so they could engage learners in a genuine way.

In the anecdote above, the classroom teacher had been two questions away from discovering the connections this student had made between the text and everyday occurrences in her life. The truth is that in many schools, the backgrounds and life experiences of teachers and students are not aligned. However, that is to be expected since we live in such a culturally blended society.

Therein lie two diverged roads that every educator encounters. The educator can either seek to know more about the learner's culture and environment and incorporate those elements into creative and critical thinking activities, or only really acknowledge the learner's intelligence when it reflects the teacher's own thinking. If the instructional leader or teacher chooses the latter, each school day begins with a handicap.

The differences in the experiences of school leaders, teachers, and students include a vast range of elements such as environment, gender, ethnicity, religious beliefs, and family values. Given these differences in backgrounds, any school district can be vulnerable to disconnects in teaching and learning.

Of course, following the lesson, the instructional leader conducted a post-conference with the teacher. If the leader had not been present in that particular classroom, the exchange that occurred between this student and teacher would not have been addressed.

How do these missed opportunities for teachers to expand learning affect the psyche of a child? They can lead children to second-guess their ability to make solid connections. This, in turn, affects a student's ability to take risks think creatively, and inhibits "out of the box thinking." In short, it creates an unnecessary obstacle to learning.

DEVELOPING PERSONAL-PROFESSIONAL RELATIONSHIPS

If school leaders want parents to actively take part in transformations, they must first recognize parents as individuals. The mindsets of parents and students need to be massaged in order to prepare them for positive changes that schools desire to make. This means taking into account the whole person and ensuring that parents and students fully understand the intended purpose of a particular change.

People want to be acknowledged, and not just in a superficial way. Many students and parents alike bring with them rich experiences and cultures, and most desire to share their backgrounds with the school. Culture is a badge of honor—an identity. Interactions between home and school should be approached with a desire to make personal connections with students and their parents. Ideally, the connections will be personal-professional.

A personal-professional relationship is characterized by a professional who intentionally sets out to acknowledge the culture of another. A personal-professional relationship does not seek to build a close friendship. Instead, this relationship is one defined by mutual respect and trust. The respect is built by acknowledging the essence of a person, while the trust is established through how the shared information gets used. For example, any information gathered from a parent should always result in tangible positive outcomes for the student.

Parents are more likely to share information when the information is utilized to improve learning for their child. It is incumbent upon the school district to make those correlations clear to parents and the community. That is to say, people don't often feel comfortable sharing personal information about themselves just for the sake of sharing. However, if by sharing the information it leads to improvements, it becomes an incentive for continued dialogue.

The school representative, whether that person is a guidance counselor, school principal, or teacher, should seek to understand the traditions, fundamental beliefs, and values of families in the context of a personal-professional relationship. It is not necessary for schools to agree with families' philosophies. However, this information is useful when schools attempt to meet the needs of the "whole" child. It is for this reason that the personal-professional relationship between the parent and the school is advantageous. Here are a few more reasons administrators should encourage personal-professional relationships:

- As schools attempt to differentiate instruction, school leaders will need to ensure that staff members understand the backgrounds, cultures, and worldviews of parent and student populations. Only then can schools truly address the specific learning styles and needs of students.
- Building personal-professional relationships with parents helps schools identify parents who are suited to serve on particular school and district committees.
- Staff members will establish a better understanding of student behaviors. For example, staff should be able to distinguish between behaviors that stem from a child's cultural background and behaviors that seek to be disrespectful. Oftentimes, due to a

lack of background information, behaviors are misunderstood and the consequences can therefore be inappropriate.

• When parents believe that their culture is validated by the school district, the line of communication is reciprocal. Conversely, when parents do not feel validated, they become less willing to participate in schools.

Many school districts hold cultural events each year. During these events, participants partake in a wide range of cultural cuisines, observe performances that are native to particular cultures, and listen to parents and students explain aspects of their heritage. These events are useful as an introduction to an individual's cultural background, but it is only the beginning of bridging cultural gaps.

Personal-professional relationships help schools delve deeper into the degrees of a given culture. There are usually several layers to each individual to uncover. The shared information and experiences between home and school can aid in the development of student creativity.

Steps for creating personal-professional relationships with families include the following:

• Many school districts disaggregate data and most are aware of the number of ethnicities represented in a respective school district, but administrators should also seek to conduct cultural background research on those individual families. This helps in the acclimation process of both staff and students.

• To ensure that families of diverse backgrounds feel included in decision making, instructional leaders should create committees that include parents who truly reflect the student population.

- Leaders need to provide professional learning to teachers to establish boundaries for forming personal-professional relationships with families. For example, leaders will want teachers to have the ability, in advance, to ask questions about any ambiguous concerns regarding building personal-professional relationships.

- At the beginning of the school year, each class should have an informal social for parents in respective classrooms. Teachers can offer refreshments. This would not be considered a back-to-school night, rather a time to focus on relationship building. Typically, back-to-school agendas focus on the goals of the district, school, and classroom teacher. An informal parent social allows parents to share aspects of their cultural beliefs about education. Administrators will need to provide staff with ground rules for keeping such an event informal and discuss ways to avoid talking about individual student progress.

A Framework for Creativity

Educational leaders inherit the task of encouraging teachers to prepare students to think outside the box, but teachers themselves must first display these attributes in their own work. Developing strong creative and critical-thinking skills in staff is essential, as each individual in the field of education is at various stages of mastery. Consequently, creative thinking for both staff and students needs to be nurtured.

Children begin their schooling careers with unlimited imaginations. Many of us have observed children's rapid decline of creativity as they work their way through the K–12 system. Leveraging and fostering children's natural curiosity and creative thinking skills early on in the schooling process is a productive approach to ultimately sustaining creativity. Most importantly, we need teachers who recognize creative and critical-thinking skills in learners, and who can channel those skills appropriately.

Effective teachers promote teaching strategies that encourage the imaginative and innovative spirit children bring to learning. There are many teachers in education who are creative thinkers and flexible in their instructional delivery. Unfortunately, not all teachers are equipped with a creative or critical-thinking skillset, and those teachers who successfully foster creativity in students are not always embraced or acknowledged by school leaders for their distinct instructional styles.

Leaders cannot expect teachers to recognize and nurture creativity in students if creative thinking is not embedded in the framework of school culture and held in high esteem. Teachers do not need to possess talents equivalent to Picasso or Shakespeare, but they do need to be able to implement strategies that promote thinking outside the box, and well beyond that realm. Teachers who develop acute listening skills and ask the right questions of students are on a solid path to building teaching and learning rapport.

Trust between teacher and student helps create a classroom environment wherein students feel safe taking learning risks. Additionally, a trusting and open environment allows teachers to access the core of a child's thinking process. By creating such a setting, teachers become more willing to take calculated instructional risks as well.

Tips for Promoting School-Wide Creativity

1. Encourage staff across the curriculum to consistently ask students, "Are there other ways to arrive at a solution or respond to a question?" School-wide, if the focus centers on looking

at all possibilities, this paves the way for creative thinking to become second nature for students.

2. Celebrate divergent thinking. Set aside some time during the school year for teachers to share experiences about how their students demonstrated critical and creative thinking skills in class. Teachers can also describe how they maximized those moments. Sharing specific examples can help other teachers more readily recognize, enhance, and appreciate creative and critical-thinking skills in their own students.

3. Since teachers need to constantly sharpen their creative and critical-thinking skills, ongoing creative projects that provide opportunities for staff members to demonstrate their creative and critical-thinking abilities should be prevalent in the school each year. For example, staff can volunteer to contribute to in-house research, provide a series of creative and critical thinking workshops, or participate in an initiative to think of creative ways to partner with parents and community members. Ask staff to develop innovative ways to think about relevant issues.

4. Each marking period, request that teachers across the curriculum select a student project or assignment that exemplifies creative thinking. Students' work can be displayed in a designated area. Teachers should attach an explanation to each piece, preferably written by students, which explains why the project or assignment depicts creative thinking.

Creative Connections

If we want to tap into children's creativity, then we need to meet students where they are—in the digital world. Leaders are aware that the amount of television and social media content that children digest has increased steadily over the past few decades. So, how do these encounters impact children's creative thinking skills?

There are great opportunities for schools to recycle the information that students absorb from these forums to purposefully guide children's texting, television, and online experiences. Schools can help students "think beyond the realm" by educating students to think about their own thinking and habits. For example, there are many lessons to be learned that relate to the value of time and how students spend it, especially with regard to online experiences.

Effective leaders encourage educators to pose questions and assignments that guide students to reflect critically on the quality of their "connected" time. For instance, students can track how much time is spent online, texting, and viewing television, and then arrive at percentages and averages of how their time was divided. In addition, learners decide if their investment of time benefited their educational goals.

Time can easily slip away from children as they "surf the net." The average adult may lack awareness of how much time they themselves spend in front of the television or online per week. However, it is wise to raise the level of consciousness for children who are in the midst of preparing for college and a career. If children choose to spend much of their downtime in the technological world, then schools can leverage this by sharing tips and reliable websites with learners that will enhance creative and critical-thinking skills.

As children develop and take on more responsibilities in school and in life, they will need to know how to manage time and maximize their days. There are endless ways for educators to help children utilize and think critically and creatively about technology. Children spend so much time linked to the digital world that it makes sense for schools to seize teachable moments that spring from these experiences.

While educators scramble to figure out ways to keep up with and embed technology into teaching and learning, students have already discovered creative new uses for their apparatuses. Administrators can encourage the student body to contribute to the conversation regarding ways to incorporate technology into learning. This can easily be accomplished by first addressing the topic with students and then following up with a suggestion box designed specifically around this topic.

Administrators and teachers will be surprised by the ideas students can contribute. Since the average students' world is immersed in technology and its many uses, then who better to ask? This can be a great exercise in collective thinking and can provide an opportunity to massage the mindsets of both students and staff. Staff will have the opportunity to witness systemic thinking and systemic change in action as the instructional leader engages the student body in real-life problem-solving.

WHAT'S OUTSIDE THE BOX?

Outside of the box, there are opportunities for every child to experience a level of success. The balance and exchange of knowledge between educator and student guides students to think divergently. Therefore, it is imperative that school leaders and staff don't miss opportunities to further a child's thinking ability.

In the space between inside of the box and the outer realm of the box, there is a delicate area where exercises in thinking take place and, ultimately, out of the box ideas are born. It is imperative that students' ideas be processed carefully by teachers so that enhancement of children's creative and critical-thinking skills is a pleasurable experience, which will eventually lead them to challenge their own thinking.

Socrates once said, "I am the wisest man alive, for I know one thing, and that is that I know nothing." If leaders can massage the mindsets of staff so they approach teaching and learning with humility and can validate students' experiences, exploring the notion that teachers can learn from students, then the odds of moving children toward advanced proficiency will undoubtedly increase.

Too often in school districts, the focus is on proficiency—not advanced proficiency. If children are to be globally competitive, then we must proceed differently and, whenever possible, be receptive to students' existence outside the school walls.

Although it is unwritten, educational leaders have a duty to possess an understanding of the cultures, backgrounds, and interests of students and then help staff recognize the significance of these elements. All of us are a unique blend and result of our childhoods and adult experiences, whether those experiences were negative or positive. Yet, often in classrooms, children's in-school experiences are separated from their home lives.

If educators can see past themselves and begin to maximize the sometimes off-centered, but valid, viewpoints that children offer, schools would experience richer discussions in classrooms, meaningful conceptual exchanges, and there would be more students willing to demonstrate creative thinking.

COMMON ERRORS IN LEADERSHIP

Another obstacle that can prohibit progressive movement in schools is school district leadership. It is said that a man can be his own worst enemy. There are some very basic common sense approaches to leading that leaders should remember. Decision-making is the key to leadership. During the decision-making process, leaders will be faced with multiple choices. It is always prudent to factor in laws, policies, and procedures in reaching decisions.

When schools veer from these three fundamental guides, trouble ensues. There are numerous cases that depict poor decision-making skills. If simple guidelines had been followed, the decisions never would have drawn the undesirable attention to schools and school districts that they did. Collectively, the following stories act as a guide for what school leaders should avoid.

On November 12, 2013, Amy Lacey, then principal at Hempstead Middle School in Texas, announced over the school's public address system that speaking Spanish in class would no longer be allowed. The school district had a high population of Spanish-speaking students. Even though there was no policy in place in the school district to support her announcement, she made the decision to create and implement this policy on her own. Her choice commanded front-page attention in media outlets across the world condemning her decision. Subsequently, she was relieved of her duties.

In February 2014, the New York Department of Education fired Principal Marcella Sills in response to allegations and later proof that she lied about her attendance at Far Rockaway's Public School 106. The Department of Education found that she had received full pay, all the while, frequently being a no-show. This demonstrated a disregard for the law as well as for school district policies.

In 2012, in the state of Georgia, a Cobb County middle school principal, Jerry Dority, and counselor, Yatta Collins, were both terminated because they were accused of waiting too long to report a case of suspected sex abuse of a child. The state's law required that suspected sex abuse be reported to authorities within 24 hours.

Although, they did eventually report the abuse, it was beyond the prescribed time frame.

A former principal at Parks Middle School, Atlanta, Georgia, pled guilty to his role in cheating on standardized tests. The former principal, Christopher Waller, agreed to pay $50,000 in fines and perform 1,000 hours of community service. He stated in court: "I accept responsibility for this conduct which was unethical, immoral, dishonest and criminal."

To some, these cases may seem far-fetched, but all have a common theme. Each case began with an act of poor judgment—a lapse in common sense. These are examples of what happens when school and district leaders circumvent laws, policies, and procedures. Most district policies are well thought-out and take into account federal law, state law, and local union policies. Many school district policies and procedures were born out of the aftermath of unforeseen and unfortunate events, primarily in an attempt to avoid a repeat of poor leadership choices.

Common sense dictates that leaders who follow policies and procedures will more likely be successful in staying the course in moving their schools forward. The time and energy that is invested in school and district investigations derail the focus on teaching and learning and consumes valuable district resources. When staff and community no longer trust leadership, the mindsets of parents, students, and staff shift from positive, constructive thinking to negative, speculative concentration.

Building trust among shareholders often takes years for leaders to establish, but can quickly collapse with one botched decision. Therefore, it is necessary to know and consistently review regulations. Even veteran administrators can fall victim to creating pseudopolicies.

Leaders should avoid the snowball effect of bad decision-making. This occurs when more than one school district leader agrees to manipulate policies. It may seem okay to sidestep a policy because more than one individual is involved, and it may be harder for school and district leaders to resist because they want to align their actions with colleagues, but if the policies have not been officially adopted by the school, there can be much at stake.

In September 2014, a high school teacher who worked in a Tennessee school district, Angela Delozier, was awarded a settlement from the Bradley County Board of Education. She alleged that the school district mishandled a sexual harassment complaint she made against a superior. In the complaint, Delozier claimed that after reporting the sexual harassment incidents to the school principal and other district officials, she was told that her contract would not be renewed, even though she had previously received good evaluations. She further claimed that she was forced to resign.

In Columbus, Ohio, two high school principals were fired in March 2014 for their alleged participation in manipulating student records. The school board terminated former STEM Academy's Principal Tiffany Chavers and Marion-Franklin School's Principal Pamela Diggs. According to the local newspaper, *The Columbus Dispatch*, Diggs later stated, "It's not over because there is a whole other side to the story. This was a top-down scheme that took place from 2002. This is what we were trained to do, so I don't think I did anything wrong. . . . It was nothing that was ever questioned because it was across the board."

When more than one individual is involved in the bypassing of policies or simply set out to create their own policies and procedures, this crafts a slippery slope. In Diggs's statement above, she defends her actions. Her response appears to be the result of several leaders' conspiring to consciously disregard school district regulations. Even if other leaders were involved, she, an educational leader, had to know that altering student attendance and grades was not aligned with district policy.

In 2014, National Football League (NFL) player Ray Rice and his fiancée were captured on camera in an elevator engaged in a physical altercation. Initially, for his role in the domestic violence act, wherein his fiancée appeared to be rendered unconscious, Ray Rice received a two-game suspension. After public outcry that the punishment did not befit the level of violence, the NFL, a multibillion dollar business, had to rethink its policy on misconduct as it related to domestic abuse and violence.

The NFL commisioner at the time, Roger Goodell, had this to say: "At times . . . despite our best efforts, we fall short of our goals." Goodell continued, "We clearly did so in response to a recent incident of domestic violence. We allowed our standards to fall below where they should be and lost an important opportunity to emphasize our strong stance on a critical issue and the effective programs we have in place." Rice was fired. During the appeals process, Rice's indefinite suspension was later overturned, but the NFL admitted that the case has prompted the organization to reassess its policies. Regarding this incident, one of the most significant lessons organizations can learn is to review policies and procedures regularly to avoid similar embarrassing situations. With a wide range of lawyers and consultants at the disposal of the NFL, and the profile individuals connected with the organization, one might think it a regular practice of the league to review and update policies so that a reprimand fits the magnitude of an incident.

On June 22, 2012, former Penn State defensive coordinator Gerald "Jerry" Sandusky was found guilty of child sexual abuse. He was convicted of 45 out of 48 counts. He was accused of sexually abusing 10 boys under the age of 18 over a 15-year period. After the scandal broke, Penn State University fired longtime coach Joe Paterno and President Graham Spanier on November 9, four days after Sandusky was initially arrested. Two school officials were both accused of perjury and failing to report suspected child abuse. They were Athletic Director Tim Curley and Gary Schultz, a vice president, who both resigned from their duties.

Many would agree that it is difficult to fathom how adults could suspect someone of committing child sexual abuse and not contact the proper authorities. Some officials at Penn State University suspected that young boys were being molested for years at the hands of Sandusky, and a few even witnessed him in inappropriate circumstances with young boys, but did nothing. Many of these leaders claimed that they did not come forth for fear of losing their jobs or simply because they did not want to get involved. Instead, they lost far more—respect of self, family, and community. The children, who were supposed to be protected by adults, experienced losses that can never be recovered. This explosive case revealed intense layers of poor leadership and demonstrated how easily a house of cards can fall.

Tips for Adhering to Regulations:

1. The moment a leader realizes there has been a lapse in judgment, that individual should consult with the school board. Admitting to a mistake in a timely fashion and reporting it early can help the school district create a damage control plan. Given the popularity of social media, news of an event can reach the press in a matter of minutes. It is better that the

leader discuss the issue with district officials first, rather than take a chance on how the press may present it.

2. Even though the temptation arises and seems plausible, administrators should refrain from manipulating district policies and procedures to suit their immediate needs.

3. In cases of nonemergencies, if a leader is unsure about the appropriate action, the leader should simply hold off on making a firm decision until he/she has had the opportunity to research laws, policies, and procedures. Many haphazard decisions have been made in haste.

4. If a leader knows that a colleague is breaking the law, that leader has an obligation to report it in a timely manner.

5. Don't write anything in an e-mail or a text message that you do not want displayed to the world.

There are everyday issues that arise that require sound judgment on the part of school and district administrators; many will be on-the-spot decisions. For example, student behavior, walk-throughs, parent concerns, cafeteria issues, busing concerns, and security matters all require daily attention. The list is endless. Massaging the mindset does not mean that all shareholders will be pleased with the decisions that leaders make, but if those leaders strictly abide by district policies and procedures, they can diminish the probability for the breakdown of trust and increase the opportunity to pursue progressive paths in teaching and learning.

Fundamentally, solid leadership is framed by good choices. Too often leaders and staff are sidetracked by avoidable circumstances. These lead to the filing of grievances by employees. Some of the issues that drive school leaders' and other educators' attention away from the implementation of best practices are situations that clearly could have been avoided if a leader or teacher had simply used good judgment.

System-Wide Practices

When massaging the mindset, choosing the right system-wide practices to implement in schools can alleviate problems and help maintain progressive movement. It is no secret that many teachers work in silos. School districts are attempting to change the mindsets of staff through the development of small learning communities, increased common planning time, and development of teachers as leaders.

While most school and district leaders understand the need for systemic rules and regulations, the problem often lies in the implementation process. Conducting school walk-throughs alone is not enough to ensure thorough implementation of best practices. Therefore, it is prudent to introduce self-monitoring tools to staff.

Many educators strive to be masters who require insight rather than acute oversight of their craft. By providing self-monitoring tools to staff, such as a weekly checklist of best practices, this can act as a guide to implementation. Self-evaluation tools should be used frequently and discussed in post-conferences with staff.

Putting staff on a self-monitoring track will help them better measure their own strengths and challenges. It will also allow staff to self-correct in various areas of instruction. In the beginning, both teacher and school administrator should ideally agree upon the self-evaluation tool. Eventually, as they grow in some areas and find other areas that need developing, teachers alone will adjust the tool.

STUDENT BEHAVIOR

Why do some teachers excel at maintaining good behavior in classrooms, while others struggle with student behavior—so much so that sending students to the principal's office becomes a daily occurrence? Any effective school leader knows that there are basic principles to establishing and sustaining a safe learning environment; however, huge disparities from one classroom to the next often exist.

Classroom behavior has a domino effect. If negative behaviors are not addressed early in the school year, grades and summative test scores suffer. In addition, children who exhibit negative behaviors often receive the most attention from the instructor, all students endure an environment that is not psychologically healthy, students' safety is compromised, and time is wasted.

Students must be aware of consequences, and those consequences should be consistently carried through. It is not uncommon for administrators to underreport fights or assaults in an effort to present respectable numbers to the state regarding the level of violence at a given school. Administrators should be cognizant that students become aware of inconsistencies in reprimands and they can in turn make a teacher's job daunting. The fact that the administrator is not consistent in following through with disciplinary policies and procedures can create resentment on the part of the teacher toward the administrator.

Given all that can be lost in a chaotic classroom setting, a detailed, system-wide behavioral plan is necessary in each school. Since each school has a unique blend of staff, students, and parent populations, the approach to student behavior may differ slightly from school to school. However, it is wise to ensure that these variances in approach are aligned with district policies.

Ideally, staff will have input with regard to developing a plan. The plan should be targeted and researched based—based on the positive outcomes of teachers in a given school within the district who have proven to effectively navigate student behaviors. These teachers will have demonstrated success in this area with the same population of students for whom the school-wide strategies will ultimately be implemented.

A school or district can benefit from incorporating behavioral strategies into a self-monitoring checklist for staff. Most walk-through checklists center around specific instructional practices that administrators expect will be incorporated into lessons and sometimes overlook the behavioral aspect. Nevertheless, a mutually respectful classroom setting guarantees the possibility that good teaching and learning can occur. Implementing a self-evaluation tool that includes behavior is an efficient way for administrators to demonstrate the importance of behavior.

Balance plays a pivotal role in education. Therefore, all factors concerning teaching and learning demand respect. Often, staff will look to leaders to determine where to place emphasis on instructional practices. Whether verbally or nonverbally, leaders send clear messages to staff regarding what they deem are most important in the educational process.

In past years, some administrators have given teachers good evaluations based on perfectly orderly classrooms. Indeed, these teachers possessed the ability to command students' attention. However, this is similar to the quiet student who receives A's from the teacher for consistently enduring an unruly classroom setting. Irrespective of how poor student behavior may be school-wide or district-wide, teacher evaluations have to be balanced, based on multiple factors.

Undoubtedly, behavior plays a huge role in the teaching and learning progression. Still, it is not a basis for labeling a teacher effective. Teachers who have excellent classroom management skills are valuable to any school administrator for a number of reasons. One major reason is that these teachers independently handle behavioral issues, thus giving the principal more time to complete other tasks, but that alone doesn't embody an efficient teacher.

On the flip side, classroom behavior is such an important factor that it has the ability to enhance or completely deflate a lesson. So, if behavior is such an important issue, how can a principal track and support the improvement of a teacher's classroom management skills? The principal must set out to discover the root cause of a problem.

On a principal's walk-through checklist as well as a teacher's self-monitoring tool, a teacher's classroom management techniques should not simply be evaluated by one word with boxes next to it to indicate "effective" or "ineffective" classroom management. Instead, questions should address behaviors that are specific to a particular classroom. For example: Were my exchanges with students respectful? Did my lesson hold student's interest? Did I allow myself to get drawn into a verbal confrontation with a student?

These types of questions can initially be answered "yes" or "no," but still allow opportunities for focused reflection and targeted post-conference discussions to transpire. Specific questions about behavior, such as these, seek to identify underlying problems and can lead the teacher or administrator to ask other pertinent questions.

Consider the following elements when constructing a self-evaluation tool that includes behavior:

1. When disciplined, students will often believe that adults are unjustly punishing them. Therefore, they neither accept full

responsibility nor do they exercise critical-thinking skills. Good leaders make sure that staff members consistently remind students that a choice is a conscious act. Additionally, an astute question for staff to ask students is: What is the lesson to be learned from your choices? These steps shape a reflective mindset in children and help them discover life's lessons that poor choices spawn.

2. Having consistency across the school or district is paramount. Children of all ages trust that staff will be fair in their delivery of consequences for particular actions. Once that trust has been broken, it is difficult to regain. Consequently, staff cannot accept a behavior from one student, but have intolerance for the identical behavior when displayed by another. Inequity in the delivery of consequences, however, tends to be unconscious behavior on the part of staff. So, gentle reminders from administrators throughout the school year may be sufficient in correcting much of this inconsistent behavior.

3. In addition, adults may unconsciously hold grudges against children who exhibit poor behavior. After the consequence has been administered or agreed upon, move on. It is defeatist to continually bring up past incidences. Avoiding this situation will allow students opportunities for behavioral growth.

4. The school leader is responsible for making outreach to parents a priority. Administrators make a shrewd investment when they encourage teachers to reach out to a certain number of parents per week. This has been stated many times in different ways to school administrators and staff, but, ultimately, families only receive phone calls from the school when a child has caused a disruption. Schools would greatly benefit from making a conscious effort to change this method

of interfacing with families. This message will need to be consistent throughout the school year.

READING AND WRITING ACROSS THE CURRICULUM

In the shadow of science, technology, engineering, and mathematics (STEM) subjects, the focus on reading and writing skills has diminished. However, this doesn't necessarily need to be the case, as so much of any subject relies heavily on students possessing proficient reading and writing skills. For example, most educators know that mathematics scores suffer when reading comprehension is low. Additionally, when students do not fully grasp writing concepts, students have difficulty explaining mathematics concepts, history lessons, and scientific theories in written form.

Reading and writing across content areas have always occurred. Nonetheless, improving reading and writing skills systemically, across the curriculum, remains a problem in many schools. Without solid reading and writing, how could any teacher increase a student's knowledge base? The issue does not lie in getting students to write across the curriculum, because they are already engaging in reading and writing in all classrooms. The problem lies in aligning the quality of reading and writing that each teacher accepts from students. As students move from one class to the next, the expectations for reading and writing skills differ greatly and need to be aligned.

The Common Core State Standards (CCSS) demand that writing be evidence-based. In some classrooms, evidenced-based writing has always been a part of teaching and learning. For instance, science theories are based on scientific evidence. History lessons focus largely on facts and informational reading. There already exists a foundation for skill building of both reading and writing in various subjects.

Since many administrators understand that subjects and skills work in tandem, the concern becomes how to maintain a focus on all components. When taking a systemic approach to implementation, it is necessary for administrators to massage the mindsets of staff so there is widespread buy-in of ideas. How can school leaders approach this process?

1. Leaders must present a clear case for correlations between strong skill building and outcomes in subjects. Teachers frequently observe the connections between poor reading and writing skills in specific subject areas, yet blame the English language arts teachers for these gaps. Many subject-area teachers have a profound belief that they do not have an obligation to "teach" reading and writing skills. At the very least, every teacher has an obligation to reinforce skills that increase student success in all classrooms.

2. All subject-area teachers need to possess basic knowledge regarding how to improve reading-comprehension skills and writing skills. Leaders should be prepared to explain the benefit of this type of professional learning to each teacher who is required to learn related strategies.

3. Leaders can arrange for reading specialists who are already employed by the district to provide professional teaching to staff regarding how to build reading and writing skills strategically across a given district or school. This method of professional learning is cost efficient.

4. Every teacher's self-monitoring checklist should include how he/she plans to develop and reinforce reading and writing skills. Many teachers in various subject areas have writing

process charts posted in their classrooms, but teachers still need to actively assist students in developing strong reading and writing abilities.

5. Administrators can pair small groups of English language arts (ELA) teachers with small groups of subject-area teachers to share tips and strategies on how to incorporate reading and writing skill building into lessons. In this respect, small groups are better than one-to-one interfacing because this will provide an opportunity for teachers to choose from several styles and methodologies. Teachers of specific subject areas can also share strategies regarding how ELA teachers can incorporate various subjects into ELA lessons.

There has been much written about cross-curriculum instruction. Most teachers have a clear understanding of the concept but do not always communicate with a cross section of colleagues. This makes it impossible to implement such a strategy, as this approach requires ongoing cross-fertilization of ideas. The importance of this type of communication across a learning organization first has to be outlined by the leader and then frequently expressed to employees, and opportunities need to be created for staff to engage in regular cross-curriculum discussions.

SCHOOL-WIDE SUPPORT FOR NEW TEACHERS

Another major hurdle in schools can be the acclimation of new staff. If educational leaders desire new teachers to adapt quickly to a school environment, they will need to make sure that new teachers have sufficient support. Most school districts assign mentors to work with new teachers. That person is usually a veteran teacher who helps a new teacher navigate the school system—everything from planning lessons to how to address student behaviors.

However, if leaders encourage the entire school staff to extend their knowledge and expertise to new teachers, and provide a network of dependable support, a greater chance for new teachers to succeed is created. Many new teachers enter into a new school district feeling out of place, and are expected to build new relationships with students, families, and colleagues. In addition, the core duties of teaching tax new teachers.

When new teachers begin working in a district, many are met with warm welcomes from staff. However, what they need most are fellow teachers whom they can readily seek out when faced with specific issues that arise. Having a wide range of supportive colleagues who are committed to assisting new teachers provides reassurance that new teachers will quickly adjust to their new surroundings. Perhaps by forming a volunteer "Big Brother" program, schools will encourage veteran teachers to make a commitment to helping new teachers.

Students and parents expect that new and veteran teachers alike will arrive to classes ready to perform. This is a realistic expectation since in school settings there is little time for slow acclimation. Instructional time is valuable and should be maximized. District and school leaders who can find ways to provide system-wide support to new teachers can ease the anxiety associated with adjusting to a new environment.

Leaders can immediately connect new teachers to colleagues who can help them. First, leaders need to identify veteran teachers who are willing to support new teachers in their role. This can occur in numerous ways.

Whenever a new teacher has been hired, it is incumbent upon leaders to inform staff of the new addition well in advance of that individual's arrival at the school. The leader can ask staff to think of ways each can support the new teacher, and ask for volunteers who are willing to put in writing how they believe they can facilitate the new staff member's success. By implementing this method, administrators create a large-scale network for incoming staff members.

Collectively, volunteers create a pool of living resources. The volunteer list should include teachers' names, respective school e-mail addresses, and a description of how each is willing to support the new teacher. The administrator can then present a copy of the list to the incoming teacher as a quick reference of viable contacts.

Of course, new teachers will be expected to reach out to their assigned mentor as the primary point of contact when questions arise. Nonetheless, implementing a method of joint responsibility promotes collaboration among staff. This lessens the risk of isolation that new teachers often experience.

Any veteran administrator knows that once teachers have formed silos, those areas of isolation can be difficult to break down. Newly hired teachers can begin their assignment immersed in a culture of cohesiveness. Not only will this methodology massage the mindsets of new teachers, but it can also set the stage for veteran teachers to apply this type of support to other work-related situations.

Strategies for Building a Support Network for New Teachers

1. Establishing a schedule of various classrooms that a new teacher can observe throughout the school year is prudent.

The selected classrooms should reflect a variety of best practices. Since the new teacher is not evaluating the veteran teacher, but rather looking for useful strategies, the new teacher's post-conference with the instructional leader should focus solely on "takeaways"—strategies that the novice teacher plans to implement in his/her own classroom.

2. Leaders can identify teachers who are adept at reaching out to families, good at establishing trust, and skilled at maintaining relationships. New teachers need opportunities to see effective communication strategies in action. By witnessing and being able to discuss the complexities that are sometimes involved in school home relationships, new teachers can prevent major problems from forming in their own classrooms.

3. Several online social media sites contain free videos and discussions about trends in education worldwide. These can be good sources for new teachers. Social networking sites also provide a place for district staff to stay in constant communication with one another across the curriculum. When face-to-face communication is not possible, social media sites offer a viable alternative for district staff to frequently connect, giving new teachers a wide range of support.

4. A good leader extends an open-door policy to new teachers. Although most new teachers will have an assigned mentor, each will need a direct line to the school principal to establish a rapport. Building a solid rapport with new teachers is particularly important so that new teachers feel a sense of belonging.

5. Access is vital for beginning teachers. Leaders should ensure that new teachers have access to as many cross-content curriculum meetings as possible. These opportunities should not

be limited to a respective school, but should be district-wide. Additionally, new teachers should be invited to attend meetings across grade levels so that they have vertical exposure early in their teaching careers.

INDIVIDUALIZED LEARNING

Massaging the mindset does not only apply to teachers, but to students as well. Getting students to consistently raise the bar for themselves and establish high standards for their quality of work is a valuable skill to impart.

Much of individualized learning for students is supported by one-to-one conferencing in class between teacher and student about the students' quality of work. This is a time for teachers to share with children what they have observed during teaching and learning interactions, review test items, and discuss strengths and challenges. In addition, this is an opportunity for students to share with teachers how they feel about their individual progress.

Both teacher and student create a plan to advance learning. The parent role should be included in the plan, even if they can only play a limited role due to language barriers, lack of education, or other restraints. Including the parent in the plan maintains shared responsibility between home and school.

Peer conferencing is also an effective strategy for implementing individualized learning. This allows children an opportunity to reflect. Additionally, this helps children develop social skills in an academic context, build academic skills, and discuss learning in a way that is most natural and comfortable for them. Children tend to listen more attentively to one another than when they are engaged in a student–teacher conversation.

The more conversations students have with one another surrounding educational topics, the more apt they are to carry on educational conversations outside of the classroom, such as in the cafeteria, on the bus ride home, or even on the weekends. Having students discuss their work with a peer boosts confidence, as children will talk more freely and relaxed about problem areas with one another.

In a peer-to-peer feedback session a teacher can provide guidelines such as these:

- First, discuss some elements of your peer's work that was done well.
- Ask your peer what he/she thinks needs improvement.
- Help your peer develop a plan to improve his/her work.
- Ask how you can help improve his/her performance.

The above general guidelines can be applied to multiple grade levels. These guidelines leave room for students to ask more detailed questions about the actual assignment. Students should be encouraged to ask their own follow-up and probing questions. The skills to successfully navigate a peer-to-peer feedback session are developed over time with careful teacher modeling, guidance, and facilitation.

How do peer-to-peer conferences and conferences between students and teachers support the work of the instructional leader? Educational leaders consistently promote targeted assessments and individualized learning. The one-to-one settings provide a time for individual students to receive undivided attention from a peer or teacher. Rarely do these opportunities present themselves in classrooms, but when they do, there can be great value in the focused support a child receives from a peer or teacher.

As much as possible, instructional leaders should encourage and support this type of instruction. For teachers there is an opportunity to assess a child's unique needs and explore ways a particular student learns and reacts to the instructor's cues. In a peer-to-peer situation, children explore creative ideas in a relaxed setting and can act as supports for one another—perhaps less concerned about saying the right things and more fascinated about the exchange of creative ideas. Anyone who has ever observed children brainstorming together has recognized the unique chemistry that only kids can generate, and that cannot be duplicated by adult–student interactions.

Helping Teachers Individualize Learning

Many teachers are good at teaching to the middle. So it may be wise for school and district leaders to begin there. Ask teachers what skills are required to achieve successful outcomes for those students who are on grade level and who do not present noteworthy challenges. Most teachers who effectively teach to the students who fall in the middle:

- Know their content area.
- Begin every lesson with a lesson plan.
- Maintain good behavioral management.
- Reteach and retest when the majority of students do not demonstrate proficiency.
- Maintain an open line of communication with parents.
- Assess students.

A good leader acknowledges and builds on existing skillsets, and does not solely focus on the skills that an individual lacks. For example, teachers who know their content well simply need to stay abreast of trends, which can occur in-house if there are sufficient, accessible materials in place. Teachers who possess fundamental elements, but lack in specific skills, with the right diagnosis and direction, can be very effective. Thinking in this direction puts a positive slant on professional learning.

Teachers who are skillful at "teaching to the middle" can expand their fundamental talents to use the lessons they prepare as building blocks. The goal should be to make that lesson plan extraordinary. This can be accomplished by keeping students' learning styles in mind, using assessment outcomes to direct planning, and creating more student-focused lessons. Educational leaders can be instrumental in moving teachers forward using a scaffolding strategy. This approach to change is less threatening to staff.

When the leader acknowledges the teacher's strengths and simply creates a plan with teachers to strengthen those existing skills, then there is less resistance to change. On the contrary, when teachers are constantly told what they are doing wrong, the knee-jerk reaction is to push back. Every teacher has strengths. Leaders need only seek to discover those strengths.

There are times when weaknesses will need to be addressed directly. Whenever possible, taking a positive approach to corrective action creates less stress and tension for both the administrator and the staff. Oftentimes, this approach to change becomes reciprocal between the leader and staff. In particular, educational leaders view lesson plans on a regular basis, so this can be a good place to start.

Teachers need to incorporate many strategies into the lesson plan. For example, teachers should leave room for adjustments when students comprehend concepts at a faster rate than anticipated or do not catch on to concepts as quickly as a teacher may have anticipated. This is a skill that can be folded into teachers' already-existing skillsets if approached correctly.

These teachers often possess good classroom management skills. However, sometimes silence is considered orderly. Teachers will need guidance from the administrator regarding "active learning noise," as students should not be expected to be seen and not heard. Teachers who have established good rapport with students have a solid foundation for trying out effective teaching strategies like flexible grouping, project-based learning, classroom centers, and methodologies to carry out CCSS, because these teachers who are good at "teaching to the middle" have proven they can easily set parameters and students will be responsive.

Being proficient at "teaching to the middle" involves staying in touch with parents. Maintaining an open line of communication with parents is commendable, but is it always purposeful? To maximize these experiences, a leader must encourage teachers who are good at "teaching to the middle" to always have strategies to share with parents. For instance, if a child is superseding other students academically, then there need to be some alternative websites or creative assignments that teachers can provide to parents to keep students engaged at home. This behavior on the part of the teacher forces the instructor to consistently be mindful of individual student needs and the importance of partnering with parents to improve learning.

In recent years, educational leaders have recognized the gems in special education teachers as leaders of professional learning for general education teachers. There are special education teachers, special education paraprofessionals, and individualized education plan (IEP) team members who help give shape to special education students' individualized teaching and learning experiences, and who all can share experiences in aspects of differentiation of instruction and individualized learning. Calling on these individuals to coach, provide feedback, and share expertise with teachers across the curriculum creates an internal support system for implementing personalized instruction.

Teachers need to have resources available to be able to differentiate instruction. Teachers generate great ideas but without the proper resources in place, those ideas don't materialize. Not having proper access to resources lowers morale and creates an atmosphere of frustration that prevents teachers from taking risks in the classroom because they are then limited by what they can realistically accomplish. When teachers have the proper access to resources this keeps systemic change moving forward.

It is up to the administrator to ensure that teachers are well supplied within reason. Having a list of nonprofit organizations and community-based businesses that are willing to partner with a school provides additional support as it relates to both living resources and material access. With the emphasis on technology in schools, the school district leader is expected to lead the way in recommending trusted web resources that staff can utilize.

Finally, confronting obstacles in schools chiefly relies on good reflective practices and combined input from all staff members. Identifying, prioritizing, and knowing what can realistically be accomplished within a given time frame can determine how quickly systemic change occurs. Massaging the mindset—preparing staff for changes—is always the first step.

Chapter Three

Shifts in the Quality of Education

TECHNOLOGY AND CHANGE

All transitions have a point of origin—a pivotal moment of realization that things must change. Discovering that crucial point and the elements that prompt the need for change helps school leaders and staff identify and appreciate the driving force behind modifications. That stated, education has endured its share of transitions. These days, it is difficult to talk about paradigm shifts without discussing technology and how it has impacted every aspect of life—particularly education.

In order to understand the present state of affairs in education, we must revisit the past. For example, in the mid-1980s, two authors projected that technology would have a significant impact on education in the United States. In many ways, technology has enhanced our lives. Computers, as many instructional leaders are aware, can act as a wealth of information or act as a pipeline to misinformation, depending on the quality of the materials posted and the skills of the user.

The computer is just one technological medium that has majorly influenced teaching and learning. Another major contender is television. Many authors made noteworthy predictions about the impact television would have on teaching and learning. Two of those authors were Allan Bloom, author of *The Closing of the American Mind* (1987), and Neil Postman, author of *Amusing Ourselves to Death* (1985). Their theories were formulated approximately 30 years ago, and the predictions in each respective book foretold much of what U.S. schools struggle with today. Schools continuously combat the bombardment of triviality that students are exposed to on television as well as a flood of inconsequential information students garner from the Internet.

Looking at technological change in today's context, instructional leaders can relate to both Bloom's and Postman's insights. Postman (1985) outlined his concerns regarding the decline in the quality of television programming and the negative impact that media had on youth nearly 30 years ago. He also projected that television would continue to negatively impact education, writing,

> We now know that "Sesame Street" encourages children to love school only if school is like "Sesame Street." Which is to say, we now know that "Sesame Street" undermines what the traditional idea of schooling represents. Whereas a classroom is a place of social interaction, the space in front of a television set is a private preserve. Whereas in a classroom, one may ask a teacher questions, one can ask nothing of a television screen. (1985, p. 143)

Postman barred no punches when he discussed the inability of television to either shape the essence of human beings' social and emotional intellects, or contribute to the building blocks of critical thinking skills that require interaction. While television can preoccupy a child, it cannot provide the exchange of ideas necessary for growth as it relates to building higher order thinking skills. Shows like *Sesame Street* are, however, better than no exercise in learning at all. This type of program, although not the most effective method of learning for children, offers some form of instruction.

Postman (1985, p. 145) also stated, "One is entirely justified in saying that the major education enterprise now being undertaken in the United States is not happening in its classrooms but in the home, in front of the television set, and under the jurisdiction not of school administrators and teachers but of network executives and entertainers." This statement holds true today, not only for students who watch television several hours a day, but also for those who spend numerous hours per day online and texting. Entertainment as described by the *Merriam-Webster Dictionary* is "amusement or diversion provided especially by performers." This definition suggests that entertainment is not designed to act as a primary focus of an individual's life. Yet, most would agree that within the past few decades, entertainment has captured much of the public's time and attention.

The Internet inundates the onlooker with up-to-date tweets about entertainers regarding their delights, woes, fashion trends, children, significant others, and favorite foods. As it stands, there are more than a few entertainment-news programs that are televised that run for a full hour each evening. This is a good indicator that entertainers are being taken more seriously than in past years by a widespread audience.

In the past, one would hear about shocking news regarding entertainers primarily through tabloids. What was once fleeting news has now taken center stage. What are the implications to educational systems? The impact of the stream of insignificant information that dominates so much of young learners' attention is that what was once viewed as inconsequential is now dividing the time that students could spend on personal and intellectual growth and development.

Allan Bloom (1987, p. 64) had a similar take on the negative impact of technology. He believed that thinking was shaped by television programming, and that television offered a seductive substitute for traditional means of acquiring and processing knowledge. He wrote: "Lack of education simply results in students' seeking for enlightenment wherever it is readily available, without being able to distinguish between the sublime and trash, insight and propaganda. For the most part, students turn to the movies, ready prey to interested moralisms." Fast-forward almost 30 years, and Allan Bloom's depiction of media has merit—so much so that schools now teach students how to distinguish between valid information found on the Internet and information that is unsubstantiated. Also, while educators attempt to make students interested in their own realities, many students are tuning into television reality shows.

As it relates to technology, we are moving into territory in the field of education that almost compels us to incorporate pop culture into teaching and learning strategies. The competition to vie for students' attention amid myriad technological devices is great. Within the past two decades, there has been a major shift in thinking about how we deliver content. Do we "swim against the current" or do we submit to technology? Overwhelmingly, educators are choosing the latter.

Allan Bloom goes on to say, "As it now stands, students have powerful images of what a perfect body is and pursue it incessantly. But deprived of literary guidance, they no longer have an image of a perfect soul, and hence do not long to have one. They do not even imagine that there is such a thing" (1987, p. 67). Here, alluding to the decline of serious studies, Bloom refers to visual imagery and its seeming power over the written word.

Is there a correlation between Bloom's observations approximately 30 years ago and the number of cable television channels that are available in most households today? Visual imagery strongly influences youth. One clear example is the sharp rise in eating disorders among young people. According to a CNN article (2012), writer Cindy Harb stated: "A study conducted by the Agency for Healthcare Research and Quality showed that hospitalizations for eating disorders in children under 12 increased by 119% between 1999 and 2006." The article went on to state, "Experts say the problem isn't getting any better."

In a separate CNN article, 2012, Katia Hetter wrote: "Fat is the new ugly on the school playground. Children as young as 3 worry about being fat. Four- and 5-year-olds know 'skinny' is good and 'fat' is bad. Children in elementary school are calling each other fat as a put-down." Not surprisingly, at very young ages, children begin idolizing movie stars and singers. It is no secret that many performers are obsessed with their weight. As children develop, they begin emulating the images they see. Both the computer and television provide children with a barrage of what the entertainment world deems are pleasant images of males and females. Perception is often construed as truth, especially by young, impressionable minds.

There are many adults who complain that they rarely find intelligent programming on television, yet, as a norm, this technological medium is not closely monitored by parents in many homes. Technology in all its forms is so widespread that systemically, conversations and information must be shared between home and school regarding how students can gain the most from a wide range of technological resources—not just the computer.

The steady increase in cable channels and rapid decline in quality television capture the attention of our nation's children. Schools struggle to keep students focused in areas such as science, technology, engineering, and mathematics (STEM). In terms of language arts literacy, the content and misuse of the English language in television commercials and programming are many. However, this could present an opportunity for educational institutions to encourage students to identify the misuse of language in television and perhaps even earn extra credit for doing so.

School districts must take a creative approach to finding ways to incorporate learning into children's daily interactions with television, computers, and other devices. Increasingly, many educational leaders recognize what their schools are up against concerning visual technology—so much so that educational leaders consistently look for new ways to join forces with the technological world in order to better reach students and to teach from a perspective that students can attach themselves to and understand.

Are educators now experiencing a paradigm-shift regarding what some educational leaders view as a bandwagon approach to teaching and learning? The shift in question can be summed up by this famous quote: "If you can't beat 'em, join 'em." Are educators making too many concessions? The concern that many educational leaders share is not so much with the modernization of instructional delivery. Not many leaders are concerned that 20 years from now, classroom walls for many students will be in their own homes or wherever they happen to be "connected" at the moment, but instead, they are definitely concerned about the quality of teaching and learning as it relates to creating future generations of scholars.

Technology plays such a dominant role in society that it demands a place in teaching and learning. Its uses in education are endless and it has added many dimensions to various fields of study. However, not every teacher is savvy at deciding the appropriateness of technological materials, uses of devices, and selection of websites. Additionally, not every teacher possesses the ability to seamlessly tie technology into the curriculum. Therefore, educators should be discriminating as to which devices, social media sites, and technological mediums they choose to utilize at a given time.

Many teachers will embed technology into teaching and learning, but to what extent? Will those lessons be meaningful? An administrator can get excited about the prospect of a teacher incorporating technology into a lesson. However, if the injection of technology lacks purpose and if the same lesson can be delivered more effectively using a different methodology, then an alternative strategy should be considered.

As it stands, the majority of teachers in the United States feel compelled to incorporate technology into their lessons because they know that instructional leaders will often applaud their efforts irrespective of the level of depth of a lesson. Educational leaders cannot be so in awe of technology that weaknesses are overlooked in terms of how technology is being integrated.

There must be evidence of whether or not technology is effective in a given circumstance. When the use of technology is questionable for a particular lesson, the instructional leader must intervene, inject probing questions, and provide professional guidance to ensure that teachers implement technology when appropriate and in the most effective manner.

On the flip side of technology is face-to-face communication. There is no substitute for human interaction. In their respective works, Bloom and Postman both described how technology could not provide to students what face-to-face communication can.

Technology is an area that will continue to be an intrinsic part of major shifts in education. It will certainly be at the center of conversations as instructional leaders prepare for transitions in every aspect of the learning process.

CHANGE AND SHARED CULPABILITY

Shared culpability is when everyone involved in a system is attached to the outcome and share in the work. To establish shared culpability in a school, a leader must first acknowledge that all employees and partners are essential to instruction. An administrator cannot simply extend courteous behavior to teacher's assistants, custodial workers, office staff, security guards, and parents. School and district leaders must create improvement plans that include these individuals.

In a school setting, where all possibilities are born, all staff are shareholders and they are therefore a part of the intensive purpose. So, instead of respective employees having the sense of being "just a custodial worker" or "just a cafeteria worker," they directly contribute to and share in the instruction of children, as there are opportunities for instruction to occur throughout the day in myriad forms.

Fritjof Capra wrote,

> It is perhaps worthwhile to summarize the key characteristics of systems thinking at this point. The first, and most general, criterion is the shift from the parts to the whole. Living systems are integrated wholes whose properties cannot be reduced to those of smaller parts. Their essential or "systemic," properties are properties of the whole, which none of the parts have. (1996, p. 36)

Capra's description of living systems can seamlessly be applied to the educational system. The properties that the whole educational system produces cannot be duplicated by any single faction of the system.

Each child goes through an educational system is made whole by the collective efforts of all staff members. As each staff member creates scaffolds of learning for a child, that learner is transformed. Success in education does not come through the effort of one individual, or even one group of individuals, like one grade level of teachers or one group of leaders, but it is a combination of even the most unlikely contributors. For example, if a cafeteria worker, who daily encounter all students, consistently ask students what they learned each day, students would be forced to recall lessons, or if asked about the type of materials they like to read, students may look forward to telling a cafeteria worker or security guard about the books they are currently reading.

When instructional leaders think about cross-curricula instruction, administrators should consider every aspect of the school. Why not include the school nurse and cafeteria staff in cross-school conversations about health topics that can easily be connected to diet and good decision-making skills? When developing decision-making skills in students, we can certainly include school security in the conversation as well provide tangible, real-life examples of how bad choices have consequences. Office staff can contribute much to the topic of organizational skills as many administrative assistants manage hundreds of students' documents each day.

Capra goes on to state, "systemic properties are destroyed when a system is dissected into isolated elements" (1996, p. 36). Capra's statement depicts what it means to be "systemic" as he focuses on the totality of an entity. He suggests that the essence of an entity is shattered when parts are cut off from the whole. He further suggests that not only can this disconnect cause problems, but it also can lead to the destruction of a system. Given the delicate balance of a school system, those who are resistant to positive change can cause breakdowns within a system.

In order to repair the damage, leaders need full cooperation from those employees who are at the root of transformational issues. When school leaders try to circumvent the process of confronting resistant mindsets, they find themselves with larger problems. Often, a delay in dealing with issues sparks a series of complications such as overworked staff who pick up the slack for resistant staff, ongoing dissention in the organization caused by subgroups not living up to their responsibilities, and resistant staff members who become complacent because they know that leadership will not directly deal with the true, underlying issue—the mindset.

The last thing school leaders want is to be known as an enabler. However, many schools believe they can fill in the gaps that uncooperative staff members create, only to find that by overlooking staff problems or finding ways to temporarily "manage" staff issues, provisional solutions quickly fall apart. Leaders must accept that as part of their jobs they will need to face off with the mindsets of individuals in order to resolve differences regarding how transitions unfold. There are ways leaders can avoid negative exchanges while massaging staff mindsets.

Ways to Massage the Mindset:

1. Leaders can survey staff regarding the changes a school or district desires to make. The survey form should be designed to reflect staff mindsets, indicating if staff is resistant to new

transitions. The survey, in conjunction with other evidence, will give leaders clear direction.

2. Leaders can allow staff an opportunity to analyze the results of the survey, and also permit staff to present results of the survey to school and district leaders in a manner that is comfortable for them, giving staff ownership of both negative and positive reactions of fellow colleagues.

3. Leaders can present this question to staff: "Given the mandatory changes the school and district are required to make, how do we move forward in spite of some of the resistance to change that is evidenced by the survey results?" This allows employees an opportunity to develop their own ideas for combating mindset issues. After all, their working relationships involve different dynamics from the employee/administrator one, and will provide the administrator fresh insights.

TRANSFORMING THE TEACHER -EVALUATION PROCESS

There are those in the field of education who believe that the new teacher-evaluation systems that attempt to tie student success to teacher salaries are in danger of falling apart. It may be years before the new evaluation systems are perfected. There is also a possibility that the new systems may become a thing of the past, as many believe the new evaluation systems don't provide an accurate account of teacher performance. For example, Ravitch (2010) reflects on her favorite teacher, Mrs. Ruby Ratliff. She questions how Mrs. Ratliff would stand up to today's teacher-evaluation system. Regarding her favorite teacher, Diane Ravitch asks, "Would any school today recognize her ability to inspire her students to love literature? Would she get a bonus for expecting her students to use good grammar, accurate spelling, and good syntax? Would she win extra dollars for insisting that her students write long essays and for grading them promptly? I don't think so. She was a good teacher" (2010, p. 193). Ravitch discusses how a teacher's strengths might go unrewarded, largely because much of what teachers do on a daily basis is not reflected in many of the new evaluation systems. Some school districts may view the task of evaluating the "whole person" as too taxing to measure. Ravitch's reasoning is worth pondering. To what end are we assessing teachers?

Ravitch goes on to state, "But under any imaginable compensation scheme, her greatness as a teacher—her ability to inspire students and to change their lives—would go unrewarded because it is not in demand and cannot be measured" (2010, pp. 193–194). If our educational systems are to experience positive change, many instructional leaders would agree that an overhaul of dated and ineffective teacher-evaluation systems needs to be reassessed and revamped periodically. While upgrading teacher-evaluation systems is a good idea, we must do more than offer "surface" assessments of teachers. Evaluation systems that primarily focus on assessment outcomes provide a partial picture to administrators, giving a rather fragmented perception of a teacher's true impact on students.

Another notable shift is the recent attention that the field of education has been receiving from the business world. Much of it is legitimate, as it is plausible and smart for the business world to be concerned about the final products that K–12 institutions produce. The quality of education will undoubtedly affect the pool of potential employees from which the business world will draw. Therefore, the business world has its place in education.

Individuals who have worked in the business world can inform educators of what is expected of students and where the future job market is headed. In addition, business leaders can provide insight about corporate trends to help school leaders strengthen school curriculums to meet the ever-changing demands of the workforce. However, the intricate details of teaching and learning are developed skills and belong in the hands of those who thoroughly understand them.

K–12 schools can borrow concepts from the business world regarding how businesses implement effective systemic changes. Those from the business sector can provide input to schools regarding the curriculum—sharing expertise on various topics with students and staff, and providing financial support to school programs. However, post-911 brought with it a high unemployment rate and the collapse of many businesses. On the heels of this economic downturn, the field of education suddenly attracted a lot of attention from those in the business sector.

Is the field of education the new Fort Knox? For some business men and women who lost their investments during the latest U.S. recession, but who have virtually no background in education, educational ventures such as creating charter schools and educational consulting companies and assuming administrative roles in school districts have become an option. Topics such as "inner-city children" and the "quality of education" have become a platform and a business for business people who, just a few years ago, would have been viewed as unlikely experts in the field of education.

Attracting a wide range of shareholders to education has always been an attractive prospect. However, educational leaders must have the capacity to carry out many of the skills they require of teachers. Ravitch (2013) states, "Because the principal must decide which teachers will receive tenure, it is crucial that principals have prior experience as teachers and understand what good teaching is and how to recognize it. They will be called upon to evaluate and help struggling teachers."

How many other professions need to stress the importance of seeking and hiring leaders who are experienced in content, methodologies, and evaluative practices related to a given field? Ravitch's quote gives educational leaders pause because it is simplistic in nature, yet powerful because it questions the quality of leadership in education, and highlights a disturbing trend.

Like Ravitch, Pasi Sahlberg discusses in his book, *Finnish Lessons* (2011), the importance of hiring knowledgeable leaders and how Finland was able to turn around a once-faltering system by implementing this practice. The 2009 PISA results show that Finland ranks number three in the world in its overall scores in core subject areas. Sahlberg states, "In Finland, educational leadership in municipal education offices is without exception in the hands of professional educators who have experience in working in the field of education. This is an important factor in enhancing communication and building trust" (2011, p. 92).

The teacher-evaluation process is a major form of professional learning, and so it is imperative that leaders get it right. Sahlberg is certain that the key to success in school districts is expert leadership—those who are experienced at effective teaching and learning practices. Any leader who has been a teacher and who has attended various workshops remembers instinctively knowing which presenters had experience in the classroom and which presenters had little or no experience in the classroom environment. Teachers possess a sixth sense about these matters.

If teachers are convinced that a presenter had once been an effective teacher, then the connection is instantaneous. However, teachers who sense that speakers are "selling" something instinctively tune out as this is a natural reaction for any professional. Teachers will often compare notes on who they deem were knowledgeable speakers and will quickly identify those they believed were no longer in touch with teaching. These teachers don't always refer to "teacher" in the present tense. On the contrary, they often refer to the notion that once a passionate teacher, always. However, school and district leaders who remain current in best practices and who are willing to actively teach each year stand to earn a great deal of respect from those they lead.

IMPROVING U.S. SCHOOL LEADERSHIP

A significant change that could improve teacher administrator relationships is the desire of the educational administrator to be willing to partake in the fundamental "work" of educating children. As a school or district leader, even though the primary position is that of an administrator, each instructional leader should make it a point to conduct at least one demonstration lesson in a school district each year. Ideally, the lesson would revolve around innovative strategies and draw on a leader's strengths as well as involve some risk taking. The risk-taking piece is important because educational leaders will expect teachers to be risk takers and should be willing to do the same. This provides the leader insight into the discomfort some teachers feel when attempting to change their teaching style or implement new strategies.

How can one be a true instructional leader if hands-on teaching and learning are not vital parts of leadership? Demonstrating lessons to teachers once a year can keep administrators grounded, and can help leaders talk about implementation from a teacher's perspective. This is extremely important for systemic agreement in education—the ability to view change from the ground up. Instructional leaders can easily get absorbed in theory and run the risk of being "out of touch." Instructional leaders can better relate to staff if they also take on the role of teacher. This creates a lucid line of communication.

The work of educational leaders in government, both state and the federal, would benefit greatly if these government leaders were required to teach at least one class a year in a school district in the form of coaching, and required to coach building principals and district supervisors once a year. Often there is a disconnect between theory and application because leaders develop plans from snapshots rather than possess knowledge of what it is like to roll out plans day to day, taking into account today's curriculum, advanced technology, class schedules/blocks, and today's students.

Many educational leaders operate from a perspective of how teaching and learning transpired in classrooms years ago, perhaps during the time when they were teachers. It is unsettling that some school and district administrators do not possess any background in education. There are many elements of teaching that consistently change. The same is true of leadership. There have been changes in administrative law, policies and procedures, leadership models, and school reform. Yet, some government educational leaders do not actively work in school districts to experience the full impact of these transitions.

For any leader, it is one thing to read about changes in education and undergo intense professional training, but practice is where it all makes sense. A "good theory" put into practice helps a leader recognize whether or not a theory has feasibility. Due to a lack of leaders who consistently engage in the ground work of teaching and learning, much of the information that filters down from the U.S. government to the school district level is met by teachers and school leaders with disbelief or complaints that the requests from the government level are not "realistic," given the scope of the day-to-day responsibilities and work that teachers and leaders undertake. Similarly, teachers often feel the same about school and district administrators and the changes they require of them. Often, teachers feel that leaders are disengaged from the reality of day-to-day classroom instruction and do not understand what is (realistically) entailed in rolling out changes.

Irrespective of a leader's position, as stated earlier, a teacher can always sense if an administrator can carry out much of what he/she professes. When fellow educators encounter school administrators or a consultant, they can recognize within the first five minutes of interaction if that person is "authentic." Depending on the verdict, the teacher will either revere an administrator as a fellow educator or will not give much credence to the leader's advice, and if not, there will always remain an invisible hole—a ubiquitous disconnect.

It is important that leaders stay abreast of trends in education, but also be willing to model in classrooms for teachers. This helps maintain the esprit de corps of teaching and learning in a school system, and will give leaders more chances to massage the mindsets of staff. Close proximity to staff helps build trusting relationships. Staff will be more willing to learn new strategies and entertain new ideas if they respect a leader's knowledge and a good rapport has been established.

Should school districts cultivate current school leaders who do not have a teaching background? Many of these individuals will have completed an administrative program at a college or university. In some cases, while their leadership skills were honed, the teaching aspect was not. These leaders missed some very important building blocks. They missed the experience of teaching in a classroom and developing the craft of educating students, which prevents them from being their "best" in the role of educational leader. Even if leaders who lack teaching experience have made strides in a school district, there are nuances of the learning process that these administrators will never know—unless they teach.

Administrators, who were hired by school districts primarily because of their business savvy, should be required to obtain a teaching certificate. If these administrators demonstrate a commitment to improving education, then they should be supported by the school district and cultivated. In addition to acquiring a teaching certificate, these leaders would benefit greatly from mentoring by fellow administrators who possess solid teaching backgrounds, and they should also be required to teach classes each year.

An administrator who is led to believe that the classroom teaching experience is not necessary to be an effective leader in a school district, especially in roles such as superintendent or school principal, is misguided. The classroom is the frontline for educators. Every school district's successes or challenges often begin and end in a classroom setting. Therefore, it befits an educational leader to have roots in the very arena they set out to evaluate and improve. If educational leaders do not have roots in the classroom, then it is incumbent upon the school district to ensure they engage in the teaching process—not as a spectator, but as a teacher.

There are so many fragmented pieces that need to be strengthened in our systems. Being a capable instructional leader is at the forefront of change in schools. Streamlined connectivity is key. As stated by Fritjof Capra, "Ultimately—as quantum physics showed so dramatically—there are no parts at all. What we call a part is merely a pattern in an inseparable web of relationships" (1996, p. 37).

ADDRESSING THE CHANGING NEEDS OF STUDENTS

The mindset of an educator can constantly be massaged to meet the growing demands of ever-changing perceptions and changing realities. For example, the reality for many female students in the 1950s was very different from the reality and opportunities that await young girls today. Presently, there are more options for women, yet the science field sorely lacks in women researchers. Why aren't schools in general doubling efforts to promote interest for young girls in the sciences? Obviously, perceptions regarding the capabilities of female students need to change.

According to the *New York Times*,

> Researchers at Yale published a study proving that physicists, chemists and biologists are likely to view a young male scientist more favorably than a woman with the same qualifications. Presented with identical summaries of the accomplishments of two imaginary applicants, professors at six major research institutions were significantly more willing to offer the man a job. If they did hire the woman, they set her salary, on average, nearly $4,000 lower than the man's. Surprisingly, female scientists were as biased as their male counterparts. (Pollack, 2013)

There are many schools that encourage girls and promote interest in science, but not nearly enough. The Yale report offered insight into the minds of those who could welcome and nurture young women into the science fields. However, as the report revealed, those individuals don't always seize the opportunity.

The cultivation of women in the sciences has to begin in the home and in K–12 schools. The Yale report underscored the competiveness between men and women, the low expectations of women in the field, and the lack of support women can expect once they enter into science fields. It is for these reasons that promoting women in the sciences has to be an ongoing effort in the United States.

The *New York Times* article further stated,

> The new study goes a long way toward providing hard evidence of a continuing bias against women in the sciences. Only one-fifth of physics Ph.D.'s in this country are awarded to women, and only about half of those women are American; of all the physics professors in the United States, only 14 percent are women. The numbers of black and Hispanic scientists are even lower. (Pollack, 2013)

While the world changes, the mindsets of educators have to remain flexible. There are fields of study that school and district administrators and teachers need to understand in order to help prepare students for gainful employment. Some of the fields that are quickly changing and expanding are aerodynamics, the automotive industry, the creation of online businesses, "green" solutions, the technology field, and the medical industry. If educators remain abreast of the skillsets necessary to develop students who will meet growing needs in various fields of study, then children will have more options as they come face-to-face with the future job market.

The mindsets of administrators and teachers need to remain in a constant state of renewal in order to keep up with the changing needs of students. That is why "massaging the mindset" is so important. The massaging of the mindset is not a "one and done" procedure. It is constant and can occur in a variety of ways:

1. Leaders can e-mail relevant articles or quotes to staff at the start of each week, then follow up on the content during one-to-one conversations with staff throughout the workweek. These conversations can occur in passing.

2. School and district leaders can highlight the work of several staff members per month. Each staff member who is spotlighted should write a synopsis of an interesting article or book they recently read regarding a trend in education. You can post these individuals' comments and pictures online, in the main office, or in the teachers' lounge. Encourage other staff to dialogue about the topics. Create a place where comments can be posted. Instructional leaders in the district should add their comments as well.

3. Monthly staff meetings should not be dominated by the administrator, but should instead be teacher/staff centered. Leaders can allow opportunities for staff to rotate leadership roles during monthly meetings. As their colleagues can be some of their toughest critics, most will be well prepared and will conduct thorough research on a topic before presenting. Through this venue, staff members learn to respect each other's expertise, and this often leads to continued conversations beyond the meeting space.

4. Educational leaders should maintain a list of resources that staff can access. The list could include the following: schools with similar student populations that have demonstrated improvements, a list of teachers, both in the school and from other schools/districts, who are willing to mentor fellow educators, a list of parents by skillsets who wish to volunteer for specific projects, and short lists of quick tips that address issues that are prevalent in a particular district or school setting. Staff will look to an instructional leader or a district leader to help them problem-solve. Consistently steering staff in the right direction further builds trust.

The largest threat to massaging the mindset is inconsistency. Therefore, once a leader begins the process of keeping staff mindsets receptive, there needs to be a plan in place to maintain the established goals. This can appear in the form of a rotating in-house committee, a benchmarking process, a weekly/monthly checklist, or a monthly meeting with fellow administrators. Or maintenance can occur through other creative means. Whatever process the leader chooses to ensure that staff members remain enthusiastic about teaching and learning is fine, as long as massaging the mindset is viewed as a constant, key component of day-to-day operations.

Changing the mindset begins with a vision. Typically, school leaders think of professional learning as something that occurs during a workshop, through team meetings, direct coaching, and other obvious approaches. Professional learning requires skillful direction and development, and should be seamless. The leader has to believe that professional learning occurs on a daily basis, and then deliberately set out to embed the same philosophy in his/her staff. Otherwise, the leader cannot successfully massage employee mindsets, and change efforts will be fleeting.

Chapter Four

Measuring Change

FLEXIBILITY, ADAPTABILITY, AND SYSTEMIC MOVEMENT

Measuring individual flexibility, adaptability, and systemic movement in education can be tricky given the nuances that each component encompasses. One reason for this is that there are some teachers who are great dissemblers, giving the illusion of full implementation of effective practices, but their efforts are not always reflected in student performance nor are their efforts reflected in administrative observations and evaluations. However, at a glance and on the surface, their classrooms appear to mirror desired transformations.

Educational leaders know firsthand how a classroom can appear to have all the right elements intact, but the teacher hasn't completely grasped the intended changes. If this behavior is not confronted, yet another gap in education widens—that gap between proven best practices and implementation. To avoid this type of scenario, a leader must delve deeply to uncover masked weaknesses and then support teachers on their journey to change. In this chapter, we will explore the breadth and depth of transitions and discuss ways educational leaders can measure various aspects of change within staff.

Often, effective changes are not implemented in schools because there is a failure in communication between staff and school leaders. Underlying causes prevent leaders from being able to simply ask teachers to identify and verbalize the concepts they do not understand. Many leaders want to provide "targeted" assistance to classroom instructors but at times are met with "smoke and mirrors," and the professional development learning sessions made available to staff are later found to be ineffective.

If instructional leaders want to massage the mindset of individuals who teach, then leaders will need to revisit the fundamentals of psychology and remind staff of the human dynamics that all of us share and navigate through each day. Change in many circumstances in life can be challenging. Leaders can initiate focused conversations with staff in an effort to "humanize" the conversation surrounding change. This can facilitate staff in becoming cognizant of masking, help staff members take risks in spite of their vulnerabilities, and may help staff open up to leadership about shortcomings.

Each leader is at a different comfort level as it relates to dealing with an individual's thinking process. Leaders who empathize with human frailty and think about their own similar situations prepare themselves to facilitate staff progress as each employee undergoes individual transition phases. Depending upon the situation, many of us have been guilty in the past of masking, particularly in past job interviews, at one time or another. Why do some of us feel the need to embellish our skillsets?

Think back, during past job interviews when your ego was on trial and the ego protected you at all cost, with moist palms and a bit of anxiety. You wanted to be proud of your responses once you had completed the job interview and had begun that journey back to your car. So, maybe you embellished your skillsets a bit to the interviewer. When a person is being interviewed, that individual knows that an internal dialogue is imminent. We all want our internal dialogue to be one filled with confidence and reassurance. It is a well-known fact that in conversations, people will build up strengths and downplay weaknesses in an attempt to mask and cope with their insecurities.

As leaders reflect on their own past experiences with masking, it becomes clear how one can easily succumb to camouflaging their inadequacies. In many ways, teacher evaluations are similar to the interviewing process, especially in the sense that one's ego often feels pressure to please the evaluator. In addressing these types of issues, instructional leaders can apply the values that they try to instill in children and parents—to look beyond grades, and instead, focus on understanding concepts, because the giver of grades will ultimately be subjective.

If educational leaders can lead staff with this principle, they will threaten employees far less because this method strives for true excellence, not perceived perfection. How well this method is received by staff depends on the administrator's approach, which should be one of nurturing and not one that is solely evaluative/punitive. Too often individuals in organizations do not reach out for assistance, in spite of the challenges they face trying to implement practices on their own, because many anticipate a judgmental response.

There are human aspects to consider when attempting to enlist staff in the change process. Confronting the mindset requires a basic knowledge of behavior, as it is the essence of what most leaders are attempting to change. In the various roles that leaders have assumed in the field of education, many have found that by establishing some basic system-wide expectations and criteria regarding change, changes have structure and are easier to roll out.

Subsequently, understanding how the mind perceives and reacts to change is a great underpinning that is central to preparing for transitions. Once the leader and staff have a clear understanding of the mental undertakings that need to occur, the leader can introduce concrete expectations. Getting shareholders on the same mental frequency has to be the main priority.

Merriam-Webster Dictionary describes two of the fundamental abilities needed to participate in a systemic change as follows:

- *Flexibility*—characterized by a ready capability to adapt to new, different, or changing requirements.
- *Adaptability*—the ability to make fit (as for a new use) often by modification.
- *Systemic Movement*—the third core element, is generally described in a system as all components working collectively to achieve common goals.

These are three essential elements that all staff should possess. The ability to demonstrate these assets in day-to-day operations is critical if the objective is to create an environment that is conducive to change. As we attempt to identify and measure these factors, there are a few pointers to keep in mind. For instance, *flexibility* is not always typified by an individual's immediate and complete agreement to the terms of a particular change.

PERSONALITY TYPES

We should be mindful that cautious behavior can be beneficial to administrators, because leaders need staff members who can "think" beyond the steady stream of information they are presented within the field of education. So, although employees who immediately succumb to every whim are considered flexible, those who are open to innovative ideas, yet give real thought to the application of an idea before agreeing to it, should not be discounted. These are individuals in a given system who may be slow to act.

Many of these individuals seek to discover how a change will enhance classroom and school outcomes, weigh the practicality of a change, and consider the adaptability of an idea to their present circumstance. They will often become a leader's voice of reason and may help leaders avoid slippery slopes, as these individuals have the advantage of having boots on the ground, which provides them a different perspective from the school principal's aerial view. Gitlin and Margonis (1995) wrote about how those who question change can sometimes serve as indicators that initiatives are misguided.

There is also another personality to consider—the person who appears to have little to no flexibility and exhibits no interest in new ideas. It is most beneficial to approach this person from the perspective that he/she desires to deliver his/her best performance. It is not probable that people prepare themselves for work each morning, fight traffic to get there, and stay the course of a career with the sole intention of doing a poor job. Many of these people are convinced that their methodologies are efficient, or they are aware that their methodologies are dated and ineffective, but they do not know how to change and they are uncomfortable reaching out for assistance. Succinctly, there are those in educational systems who are simply cautious, and those who flatly resist. Recognizing the distinct differences between the two will help educational leaders proceed with better efficiency.

Elements of Change

Adaptability is a necessary skill that change agents must possess. It forces staff to customize a change and think critically about the culture in which they work. This makes changes more meaningful. In order to carry out a successful change, staff will need to adapt to new methodologies and various reactions to change by students, parents, and community members, as well as adopt a new template for success. These are just a few of the many transitions that accompany a single change. Needless to say, change can be an overwhelming experience. Therefore, it must be well planned and presented in a way that is crystal clear to staff. Much of how quickly staff adapts to change often depends on the ease with which they can visualize the change and more specifically envision adapting the change to their immediate environment.

Making sure *all* staff members have an understanding of flexibility, adaptability, and systemic movement, plus any additional elements that a leader deems pertinent, is a prudent move. At the very least, staff should be able to define terms associated with change using a cohesive language. Administrators can create and utilize a walk-through checklist to help gauge individual growth relative to implementing innovative ideas. Transparency should be evident as the instructional leader's vision unfolds. For example, ask for staff input when creating walk-through checklists.

Involvement in this process from a cross section of staff members is important. The checklist should be generated in collaboration with highly flexible staff, slow-to-change staff, as well as resistant staff

Figure 4.1.   Bloom's Affective Domain Chart

Category	Example and Key Words (verbs)
Receiving Phenomena: Awareness, willingness to hear, selected attention.	**Examples**: Listens to others with respect. Listens for and remembers the name of newly introduced people. **Key Words**: asks, chooses, describes, follows, gives, holds, identifies, locates, names, points to, selects, sits, erects, replies, uses.
Responding to Phenomena: Active participation on the part of the learners. Attends and reacts to a particular phenomenon. Learning outcomes may emphasize compliance in responding, willingness to respond, or satisfaction in responding (motivation).	**Examples**: Participates in class discussions. Gives a presentation. Questions new ideals, concepts, models, etc., in order to fully understand them. Knows the safety rules and practices them. **Key Words**: answers, assists, aids, complies, conforms, discusses, greets, helps, labels, performs, practices, presents, reads, recites, reports, selects, tells, writes.
Valuing: The worth or value a person attaches to a particular object, phenomenon, or behavior. This ranges from simple acceptance to the	**Examples**: Demonstrates belief in the democratic process. Is sensitive toward individual and cultural differences (value diversity). Shows the ability to

more complex state of commitment. Valuing is based on the internalization of a set of specified values, while clues to these values are expressed in the learner's overt behavior and are often identifiable.	solve problems. Proposes a plan to social improvement and follows through with commitment. Informs management on matters that one feels strongly about. **Key Words**: completes, demonstrates, differentiates, explains, follows, forms, initiates, invites, joins, justifies, proposes, reads, reports, selects, shares, studies, works.
Organization: Organizes values into priorities by contrasting different values, resolving conflicts between them, and creating a unique value system. The emphasis is on comparing, relating, and synthesizing values.	**Examples**: Recognizes the need for balance between freedom and responsible behavior. Accepts responsibility for one's behavior. Explains the role of systematic planning in solving problems. Accepts professional ethical standards. Creates a life plan in harmony with abilities, interests, and beliefs. Prioritizes time effectively to meet the needs of the organization, family, and self. **Key Words**: adheres, alters, arranges, combines, compares, completes, defends, explains, formulates, generalizes, identifies, integrates, modifies, orders, organizes, prepares, relates, synthesizes.

Internalizing values (characterization): Has a value system that controls his/her behavior. The behavior is pervasive, consistent, predictable, and most importantly, characteristic of the learner. Instructional objectives are concerned with the student's general patterns of adjustment (personal, social, emotional).	**Examples**: Shows self-reliance when working independently. Cooperates in group activities (displays teamwork). Uses an objective approach in problem solving. Displays a professional commitment to ethical practice on a daily basis. Revises judgments and changes behavior in light of new evidence. Values people for what they are, not how they look. **Key Words**: acts, discriminates, displays, influences, listens, modifies, performs, practices, proposes, qualifies, questions, revises, serves, solves, verifies.

http://www.nwlink.com/~donclark/hrd/bloom.html

members. It is particularly important that resistant staff be included in every step of the change process. Regardless to how slow some individuals are to change, be reminded that they, more than others on your staff, will need constant exposure to change-related details.

Sharpening Change Skillsets

Change can and should be approached as a science. Therefore, it is necessary to concentrate on flexibility, adaptability, and systemic movement as these factors help ensure an educator's long-term ability to make meaningful transitions. For example, in some education circles, aging teachers are frowned upon with bias because there are instructional leaders who believe these teachers lose their teacher effectiveness and become less viable as time passes. However, if teachers at all levels of experience are exposed to the proper systemic change elements, and if there are accountability instruments in place to measure these traits, we can increase the level of participation as it relates to collective change.

Table 4.1. Flexibility, Adaptability, and Systemic Movement

Flexibility	Adaptability	Systemic Movement
This individual asks how he/she can assist the educational leader in rolling out new initiatives	Driven by student data, this person can articulate ways to adapt new initiatives to enhance student outcomes	Volunteers to assist the school leader and colleagues in overcoming challenges that impede change
Exhibits the ability to exchange ideas with others and can change one's own ideas in lieu of more feasible ones	Demonstrates that lessons learned from past trials and errors can be applied to new circumstances	Actively collaborates with colleagues to come to a consensus about how to move ideas forward
Speaks positively about transitions	Figures out, articulates, and demonstrates how transitions can best benefit colleagues and students	Helps motivate other staff members to buy into change
Demonstrates the ability to change strategies when needed	Identifies when a change in strategy is necessary and adopts new strategies which target specific issues and improves outcomes	Models procedures, and discusses and clarifies information with staff members to help move initiatives forward
Shows enthusiasm for applying new knowledge	Applies new knowledge appropriately	Studies educational trends and topics independently and openly shares knowledge with school administrators and colleagues

Here are some examples of behaviors that exemplify the terms flexibility, adaptability, and systemic movement in education.

These three elements follow a natural continuum. While leaders are grooming staff to be flexible, the natural progression and integration of a similar skill is *adaptability*, which brings real purpose to transitions. Adaptability is pivotal in deciding the type of impact change will have on a school system. If a proposed transition is not compatible with a school's culture, curriculum, and student needs, then calculated adjustments will be required. The proper adjustments can only be made if a skilled staff understands how to adapt changes to a set of given circumstances. Ideally, to ensure systemic movement, administrators want staff to be able to share ideas with colleagues. While flexibility, adaptability, and systemic movement work seamlessly together, these characteristics often need to be openly discussed, refined through professional development, and modeled.

Effective leaders lead by example. Good leaders demonstrate to staff on a daily basis how flexibility, adaptability, and systemic movement are crucial components of day-to-day duties. School leaders will need to provide concrete examples. When leaders show staff how these elements can be implemented, leaders impress upon staff the importance of embedding the same qualities in the staff's own daily responsibilities.

Bloom's Affective Domain is also a relevant tool by which to measure systemic movement. The affective domain (Krathwohl, Bloom, and Masia, 1973) addresses a wide range of components that captures the mindset of an individual, including emotions, values, and attitudes. The five major categories can be seen in figure 4.1.

BREADTH AND DEPTH OF CHANGE

Since K–12 education impacts every aspect of humanity, including but not limited to incarceration rates, unemployment rates, the ecosystem, advancement in the sciences, tolerance of others, politics, and the arts, it is imperative that instructional leaders include a wide range of partners in not only decision making, but also the implementation of best practices. Schools have a responsibility to society at large, to the extent that schools need to continually find ways to expand the breadth and depth of inclusiveness. As it stands, many schools already include family and community members on myriad planning committees, and parents are often invited into initial conversations about proposed changes. However, there remains a segment of stakeholders whose potential as partners is overlooked.

Not all partnerships that are inclusive of family and community members are meaningful. Utilizing family and community members to participate on committees is great, but how do we include them in change beyond that role? In addition, internal partnerships often need to be redefined. For example, how is "peripheral" staff perceived? How effectively are they used?

THINKING STRATEGICALLY ABOUT FAMILIES
AND COMMUNITY MEMBERS

From a parent's perspective, schools can be difficult to navigate and often intimidating. With all that we know about the positive impact that collective efforts have on the implementation of initiatives, some division between school districts and those outside the school walls still remains. This division can occur for many reasons, such as limited transparency, politics, top-down management, lack of outreach, miscommunication, aloof staff, and a multitude of other issues.

There are many administrators hard at work to eradicate these divides. Efficient administrators are aware that the school perimeter extends far beyond school grounds, and thus the school day doesn't end at the sound of the bell. Much of what teachers impart to students on a given day will carry over into children's' home lives in the evenings, and all school districts hope that a child's acquired knowledge will be applied to real-life situations that often transpire away from school grounds, making the home a good breeding ground for learning. This application of knowledge can occur with more depth and meaning if families and communities are aware of school goals, have knowledge of best practices, and understand how to facilitate learning.

At a workshop for school leaders in Holland on how to strategically utilize family and community members in school systems, this poignant question was raised to the American presenter: How can the ideas you are proposing fit my school culture? The participant went on to outline anticipated obstacles such as Dutch and American cultural differences as they relates to the extent of parental involvement in schools. A school is like a thumbprint—each one is distinct. So, the question of how proven strategies can be utilized in a particular school climate was a question worth asking, and is the type of question that leaders must continually put forth.

Anytime an educational consultant is invited into a school district to improve outcomes, the leader should discuss the needs in the context of the school environment, including diversity of families and community members, and request that services be tailored to pinpoint and directly address specific needs. It is perfectly reasonable to request that an educational consultant present plans to the school district that have a breakdown of proposed methodologies and an outline of how those actions will positively impact shareholders, keeping families and community top of mind as the school provides professional learning services to staff. Any plans that are presented to a district or school from an outside entity should always be presented with the understanding that the plan will be taken under advisement and may require changes that will best benefit the school and community. Subsequently, the school leader and a diverse committee should review plans and add or detract from those plans in the best interest of the school district. This is one way to ensure that family and community are a part of the fabric of change.

Families

Parents can be a great source of support for educational leaders. If properly cultivated, educated about best practices, and given myriad opportunities to partner with schools, they can have an invaluable impact on school improvement. When parents work cohesively with school leaders, they help make desired changes in schools occur swiftly. Too often, the power of parents as "teachers" is underrated. As educational leaders, we must include parents in the teaching and learning process—not merely to assist children with homework. Parents should also be equipped with strategies that support classroom instruction, challenge students to think critically, and help move students to the next plateau.

Many parents desire to be more involved in schools, but are often intimidated by teachers and educational leaders, have busy schedules, or are simply unsure about the extent of their role in their child's education. Administrators must continue to explore ways to break down the walls that divide and consider broadening the breadth and depth of the inclusion of parents so that schools can better meet the needs of students. Several effective practices help foster parent involvement in schools.

Helpful Tips

- Share information with parents, especially regarding best practices, as this will help parents to engage in more meaningful conversations about educational topics with teachers and educational leaders.
- Hold parent meetings at varied times of the day and during different days of the week to accommodate parents' wide variety of busy schedules.
- Provide good service to parents. The first people who greet parents at the school (often the receptionists) should be friendly, knowledgeable, and welcoming.
- Periodically, ask staff to create authentic, short, and easy-to-read articles regarding educational trends and make those articles available to parents. These articles can be displayed in a parent newsletter.
- Make available at the school books, magazines, journals, videos, and Internet access if parents want to learn more about a particular educational topic. There should also be a place in the school designated as a site for parents to meet and exchange ideas.
- Make it a point to express your gratitude toward parents for their participation. An inexpensive "thank you" card adds a personal touch and lets parents know their time and efforts are appreciated.
- Provide acessibility to educational leaders. Parents need to feel secure in the fact that, although you may not always agree with their perspective, at least you make yourself available and allow parents an opportunity to be heard. Sometimes, that is enough.

• Organize a meeting that includes school and nonprofit family agencies to find out what effective practices they employ to increase parent participation. This can be accomplished in a round-table discussion wherein each participant is expected to arrive with at least one innovative, successfully implemented idea.

Community Members

Populations such as future parents, senior citizens, and school critics can all be called upon to support school goals. These groups bring with them valuable ideas and a wide range of perspectives that can strengthen any school district. Most importantly, these groups are invested in their communities and view local schools as a central part of their neighborhoods.

Schools benefit from partnering with a breadth of community members such as local business owners, nonprofit family agencies, local sports leagues, community and four-year colleges, corporate businesses, and homeless shelters. School administrators should cast their nets far and wide. Utilizing community members can help offset expenses and can enhance one's curriculum. For example, local hospital staff may have professionals on hand such as researchers who can talk to students about current research and the future of science and technology in the medical field.

These professionals have been known to come into classrooms and lead science discussions and demonstrations—connecting a classroom lesson to their real-life professional experiences. These types of interactions can occur more frequently than just on Career Day in schools. If paired with the right classrooms, co-teaching could take on a new meaning. Although these partners are local, they still lead busy lives and may need to connect with classrooms electronically. Irrespective of how they agree to take part in the teaching and learning process, partnerships like these add depth to educational experiences. Family and community members want to support school districts in a variety of ways, but are often untapped resources.

While getting the community to participate in special events is fine, we also need community members who understand the curriculum, and who support districts in implementing it. Therefore, leaders should look for ways to share curriculum content with community members. This can be done by holding a Celebrate Education Night, or whatever catchy title a school believes will attract community members. Community leaders can be essential in helping to organize events such as these. An administrator can review parts of the curriculum with local partners and then ask community members to brainstorm ways they can assist in supporting the school's initiatives. Administrators will harvest eclectic ideas. Frequently, useful ideas are born out of such discussions.

Increasing Family and Community Participation

Securing an audience is often a problem for leaders. One way of increasing parent participation is to provide incentives to students, asking them to encourage their parents to attend events. For example, students may have an opportunity to choose from several school supplies, sweatshirts or tee shirts that display school logos, or a homework pass contingent upon their parents' attendance rate at a designated number of events. Whatever the reward, it will need to be appealing to the student body.

Another method known to work in school districts is to award or honor students and parents at school events. Other family members will attend school events to support their loved ones. Parents are rarely recognized for their efforts, so if schools can find ways to celebrate parents, this can help strengthen relationships between home and school. Although parent and community participation may not increase overnight, it is imperative to continually strive to improve participation, as there is much to be gained from these alliances.

While sending out e-mail announcements is one means of disseminating an invitation to family and community members, the personal touch adds a different dimension to connecting with these groups. Increasing adult attendance at school meetings requires creativity, which often means engaging in face-to-face interaction with the community. When planning conferences, meetings, and workshops schools should try going door-to-door, handing out announcements to local businesses, churches, family agencies, libraries, and homeless shelters. Leaders may be surprised at the gratitude directors of outside agencies and homeless shelters exhibit when approached by the school district, as these establishments are often overlooked and may not regularly receive up-to-date announcements about school and community activities.

Schools should make hard copies of announcements and other pertinent information and deliver that information, either by mail or hand delivery, to the local shelters. This entity can be a pipeline to parents who are otherwise "difficult to reach." Remember, people who reside in homeless shelters are often proud families, and many of the children are sworn to secrecy about their present living conditions. That stated, it would behoove any school administrator to identify where homeless shelters are located in their respective area and maintain an open line of communication with these dwellings. In a depressed economy, homelessness is occurring in areas that school administrators may least expect, so irrespective of how affluent or low-income a district may be, leaders would be wise to connect with these facilities.

Maximizing Living Resources in Schools: A Collective Effort

In the face of budgetary challenges, how do educational leaders stay the course and accomplish goals of high performance and full implementation in areas such as science, technology, engineering, and math (STEM), language arts literacy, as well as sports and the arts? Irrespective of how many successes we have experienced as educators, still we feel the need to continuously broaden our scope and accomplish more, even in the face of economic hardships. Subsequently, we, as educational leaders, look toward already acquired and established school resources to compensate for a lack of funding.

Effective leaders understand that there needs to be a plan in place to change mindsets—shifting staff mindsets from monetary, external solutions to more grounded, internal problem-solving, as we attempt to preserve excellence in education. Most leaders will agree that effective change in school systems, or any system for that matter, occurs more efficiently when change efforts are cohesive. Maximizing untapped potential in staff is quickly becoming a viable solution to budgetary deficiencies. This cost-efficient approach to change can lead to substantial, long-lasting transformations, and if executed as a school-wide effort, can be applied swiftly.

True systemic change, by its very nature, challenges us to expand and build capacity through the effective use of living resources. Let us reflect on the average school district for a moment. Do teacher assistants, security guards, cafeteria workers, secretarial staff, and custodial workers all share common visions and educa-

tional goals with school districts? Think about the significant impact support staff can have on student success as these employees
interface with students throughout the school day. These daily encounters connect support staff with students and can be positive,
meaningful interactions, particularly if noninstructional staff is prepared and conscious of the opportunities for "teachable moments."
This is where professional development training, whether in-house
or outsourced, can be powerful. Noninstructional staff can be
trained how to effectively support classroom instruction. These
staff members could support everything from academic and social/
emotional goals to helping improve school climate.

As stated earlier in this chapter, the success of a systemic change
is measurable and can be assessed in numerous ways. In addition to
previously outlined measurement tools, a school district can measure the success of a systemic change by using indicators such as
academic achievements, shifts in school climate, leadership
growth, and instructional shifts. Additionally, breadth and depth of
change should be largely considered—meaning the extent to which
a school is willing to be inclusive. This entails viewing all employees as core staff, which can ultimately augment learning. In the
fourth edition of *The New Meaning of Educational Change*, Mi-
chael Fullan suggests that schools should work toward breaking
down barriers.

Suggestions on how to include noninstructional staff in change
efforts include the following:

- Explain school goals to noninstructional staff in layman's terms.
  Any successful advertising company will tell us that using unin-
  hibited, simplistic language to describe technical terms and concepts is the most effective means of communication for reaching
  a diverse audience.

- Allow noninstructional employees an opportunity to brainstorm how they might contribute to changes that are aligned with school goals. This fosters creativity and ownership among staff.
- Abandon the topical layer of change, thinking more in terms of a well-rounded cohesive approach that breaks down barriers between instructional and noninstructional employees.

Maximizing and mobilizing instructional and noninstructional staff toward a cohesive trajectory is a wise investment. Accomplishing this goal requires in-depth reflection regarding how the school or district presently views the term *systemic*. For example, if school staff members have extremely varied ideas regarding the meaning of the term *systemic*, then it is incumbent upon leaders to ensure that there is a consensus about the term and its usage school-wide. Otherwise, staff members will move forward based on their own individual perceptions of change. This can create confusion for leaders as well as those they lead.

Since students ideally drive the mission and goals within a given school district, they then are considered the nucleus. Therefore, it stands to reason that the surrounding entities are all positioned to support students in their learning experiences. However, this is not always the case. Typically, when superintendents and other school leaders desire to implement changes, the target audience often includes district and school administrators, teachers, and sometimes teacher assistants in isolation from other employees.

This common practice can largely be attributed to the familiar strategy of professional development in education that traditionally focuses on teachers and school principals. Succinctly, this approach is indicative of limited breadth and depth and it is not consistent with a cohesive change model, which is more inclusive. Transparency on a large scale plausibly leads to more support and paves the way for effective implementation of strategies that work. For example, sharing statistics and academic goals with both instructional and noninstructional staff members, as well as with parents, can be a catalyst to widespread change.

Many noninstructional staff members and other relevant partners in education may not be aware of summative school and district test scores. Sharing summative data with noninstructional staff in uncomplicated language may inspire those staff members to take an active role in helping improve the quality of education. Superintendents, school leaders, and teachers will be surprised at the gems they will find amid noninstructional employees—everyone from military veterans who can share their experiences with students to artists with hidden talents. The possibilities are limitless.

One clear example of finding a treasure trove among staff occurred in 1976 when a young cadet discovered that Mr. William "Bill" Crawford, a janitor at the U.S. Air Force Academy at the time, was a Medal of Honor winner. The discovery that this janitor had at one point in his life earned the Medal of Honor turned out to be a lifelong lesson for the cadet who stumbled upon the information, and it changed the subsequent conversations and interactions between the cadets attending the academy and the janitor, Mr. Crawford. He possessed firsthand knowledge of battles and other military experiences that the cadets had only read about in books, but this living resource presented a rare alternative to textbook teaching and presented potential support for the implementation of best practices at the U.S. Air Force Academy. This was an opportunity to engage staff (instructional and noninstructional) and students in the systemic thinking process.

Another inspiring story that also portrays collective thinking at its best was reported on NBC Nightly News in the spring of 2010.

A Florida school bus driver had an idea to support district reading initiatives by encouraging students to read on the school bus, thus creating a "library on wheels." She asked students to turn in book reports, and rewarded students after they had completed a certain number of books. This project helped support learning in the classroom while at the same time sent a message to students that learning neither begins nor ends at the sound of a school bell. The school district supported the bus driver's efforts. The reward for the district—priceless!

Mr. Willie Davis, a school janitor who worked at Midvale Elementary School in Tucker, Georgia, was diagnosed with cancer during his employment with the school district. Surprisingly, after his death, the school in which he worked discovered that he had left a third of his insurance benefits, $12,716.64, to the first-grade special education class in the school. With the money, the school purchased video equipment, educational materials, and prizes to reward students for their accomplishments in class. Mr. Willie Davis played a key role in supporting educational goals and encouraging students to put forth their best effort. The inheritance he left symbolized his dedication to education and the school itself. He was an intricate part of a learning community.

There are heroes among us in schools who will never be recognized in the history books, but the support they provide to educational goals are immeasurable, and if carefully developed can facilitate school districts' providing a quality education to students of limited funding. Economic recessions often prompt people to take stock of their "silos" and determine how to maximize inventoried resources. Living resources in our schools, such as teacher assistants, custodial staff, secretarial staff, security teams, school bus drivers, and cafeteria personnel, in many instances, are able and willing to support educational best practices but are often over-looked. Strategic leadership that is inclusive of support staff can make a significant difference in how well a school district sustains best practices during economic downturns, and it can also help define the roles and purpose of individuals working in school settings. Making swift, cohesive changes can often be as challenging as tackling budgetary issues. It provides some comfort to know that while school district budgets have become more restrictive, we can still find opulence in living resources.

Chapter Five

Steering Saturated Changes in Education

LAYERED TRANSITIONS

In recent years, major changes have abounded in education. In many school districts in the United States, there have been shifts occurring regarding teacher-evaluation systems; the Common Core Standards, science, technology, engineering, and mathematics (STEM) to (STEAM)—which now includes the arts; standardized testing; and a paradigm shift in the delivery of instruction. With all these changes, it is easy to understand why teachers, administrators, students, and parents are overwhelmed. So, what is the best way to navigate this flood of changes?

When leaders disaggregate, categorize, and strategically combine information to demonstrate relationships and trends, staff more easily recognize connectivity among initiatives. Information related to changes must be presented in a style that is user-friendly and outlines the overlapping end goals. When leaders are faced with multiple major transitions, the best solution to successfully managing these shifts is to organize and synthesize the data, making it more comprehensive for shareholders.

Categorizing the details of each change allows the administrator and staff to determine how multiple changes can be grouped together. Orderly arranging of the information provides the leader a clear vision regarding how to address compound transitions. Many changes in a school district feed off one another, making it easy to fold the implementation of one initiative into another.

Being aware that changes in education often cross-pollinate is an asset to educational leaders that can be strategically leveraged. For example, the Common Core State Standards (CCSS) and teacher-evaluation systems are intertwined. While states are preparing to implement teacher-evaluation systems that are directly tied to student outcomes, there are many other related factors to consider. Even states that are not yet "tying" student outcomes to teacher evaluations primarily evaluate teachers based on how well they reach goals outlined in learning standards—whatever those standards happen to be at a given time.

Student outcomes and teacher evaluations in many states are dependent upon the validity of both the CCSS and summative tests that school districts use to measure mastery. All these systemic factors undoubtedly intersect. Streamlining initiatives can make implementation seem plausible and less cumbersome to staff.

An important question that arises when educational leaders are faced with a multitude of changes is this: Where do we go from here? Since the CCSS is central to many current changes in U.S. school systems, it is a good starting point when considering other related changes. Staff will need to familiarize themselves with the intent of the CCSS.

The CCSS, which many states have adopted, seeks to improve rigor. Schools and parents will need copious hours of coaching to blend the underlying intent with a child's background knowledge, culture, and environment. There are always strategies that schools presently implement that fit seamlessly into new goals. When educational leaders hear the term "new initiative," some perceive this to mean that all new strategies will follow. As much as possible, a leader should seek to maintain effective strategies that children are accustomed to and that support new goals.

For businesses that sell educational services and products to schools, the change process can be a lucrative one. Conversely, the change process can be economically sound for prudent educational leaders. The amount of funds spent largely depends on the educational leader's mindset. Often a school administrator will need to massage his/her own mindset in order to rethink and redesign professional learning for staff.

Increasing rigor in U.S. schools has been at the center of change in education in recent years. Substantive change first occurs mentally. Well before leaders attempt to massage the mindsets of others, massaging one's own mindset as a leader has to occur. Leaders need to be in a mental space where they maintain high expectations of themselves, staff, students, and parents and can see potential in the school community even when others cannot.

Since in-house professional development is always the most cost efficient, administrators who wish to take this route should have an open discussion with staff about changes—pros and cons—and collectively figure out how to transition cons into pros given the school culture. The educational leader will need to identify staff members who have demonstrated a strong aptitude for implementing a particular initiative, make sure that staff members have access to up-to-date materials on related topics, and find ways to be inclusive of those who are less enthusiastic about the change.

Administrators can learn a great deal about change by examining the steps that were taken to create and implement the CCSS across the United States. This was a bold and major shift in American education. Does the CCSS act as a good model for how systemic change should unfold in education? To answer this question, one needs to look closely at the development of the CCSS.

Items to Consider

- Inclusiveness—What was the extent of inclusiveness during the developmental stages of the CCSS?
- Background of Committee Members—The background knowledge and accomplishments of committee members should be appropriate for the job at hand. In addition, backgrounds of members and the decisions they make should hold up under public scrutiny.
- Public Relations—Was the public well informed about the initiative?
- Purpose/Intent—If the purpose for rolling out a systemic change in education has a hint of monetary gain for particular parties, it can taint good intentions of an initiative. Politicians often live by the saying, "Perception is the truth."

As school districts unfold their own systemic changes on a local level, many will look to the major systemic changes in education that have unfolded in the last decade—that attempt to connect schools nationwide. When school administrators reflect on the CCSS and the numerous changes associated with it, there will be some significant lessons to be learned by educational leaders.

A pertinent question for leaders is: Was the proper foundation laid for rigor to occur in U.S. classrooms? If children do not have the proper foundation intact to navigate rigorous classwork, then rigor transforms from *challenging* to *impossible*. Similar to hiking, rigor is meant to be a gratifying experience. When one hikes, figuring out the best paths, footing, and ways to reserve strength is worth the effort once the hiker has achieved his/her goals, reaching a targeted plateau. That stated, rigor is intended to be rewarding—not a demeaning experience.

However, if children cannot find satisfaction or connectivity in the strategies and projects associated with rigor, then the learning process can have a failed effect. Although foundational skills are outlined in the CCSS K–5, there remain scores of children who will struggle to master basic skills beyond grade 5. What are the implications for these low-performing students? Efficient leaders know there are many negative connotations associated with students who struggle academically.

Low-performing students often feel pressured to keep up with their peers; they exhibit low self-esteem in classes; many endure feelings of frustration and demonstrate anguish; and some children believe they are less intelligent than their higher-achieving counterparts. As a result, rigor without consistent skill building, connectivity to learning, and proper supports can be detrimental to these learners.

A key part of an administrator's job in education is to advocate for students at varying levels of learning ability. Therefore, educational leaders are obligated to guarantee equity in the teaching and learning process for all students. This requires school leaders to guide teachers toward teaching and learning strategies that transform each learner, whether that learner is below proficient, within the proficient range, or considered above proficient. Given all the controversy surrounding the CCSS, educational leaders will need to devise a plan for rolling out teaching and learning that meets the needs of their population of students.

COMMON CORE STATE STANDARDS:
THE CONTROVERSY

There are questions regarding the CCSS and why the new standards were created. There are those who oppose the CCSS. One reason for this opposition is that some believe that the standards were created at the hands of predatory corporations that set out to streamline educational materials on a national level primarily for profit. If that argument were true, how would these vested companies stand to benefit?

To begin with, basing curricula across the nation on one set of unified standards conceivably decreases the time and cost involved in producing educational materials. There would be little need to adjust instructional materials in order to fit the requirements of individualized state standards. The profits that companies stand to gain from sales of testing materials that align with CCSS can be enormous.

Another popular concern regarding the development of the CCSS was the possibility that there had been U.S. government influence as well as financial backing from the federal government. This speculation stemmed from the fact that the two major organizations that agreed on the development of the CCSS are headquartered in Washington, D.C. These organizations are the National Governors Association Center for Best Practices and the Council of Chief State School Officers.

In 2009, a $4.3 billion grant, Race to the Top, was introduced by The U.S. Department of Education (USDOE). States vied for the grant money by adhering to a list of measures outlined by the USDOE. Among the criteria was the adoption of the Common Core standards. By the year 2010, this incentive led many states to adopt the new standards.

The federal government supplied $350 million to two groups. Those funds were provided to Partnership for Assessment of Readiness for College and Careers (PARCC) and Smarter Balanced to create testing materials that would align with the CCSS. The contract to produce the PARCC testing material went to Pearson Publishing Company, while CTB/McGraw-Hill won the award to produce the testing materials for Smarter Balanced Consortium.

With many critics of the CCSS subscribing to the notion that this initiative was developed top-down rather than based on local level input, there is an argument among critics that the flow of information during its inception was not fluid enough. Some believe this is why, years after its development, it received extensive backlash. By 2014, the arguments had reached a fever pitch, as evidenced by an explosion of social media postings and exchanges around the topic of CCSS by school administrators, teachers, and parents. Many of the comments were negative in nature.

Also, there are those considered experts in their fields who were asked to give their stamp of approval on the CCSS, but ultimately rejected the final version of the standards. Five out of the twenty-nine members on the CCSS Validation Committee refused to sign off on the standards' effectiveness. The fact that members of the CCSS Validation Committee were not willing to certify the document further fueled skepticism.

So, what were some of the concerns of those committee members who refused to sign the CCSS Validation document? Dr. Sandra Stotsky, a leading authority in English language arts standards and member of the CCSS Validation Committee, raised questions about the selection process regarding the developers of the CCSS, alluding to the fact that the committee lacked content area expertise. Dr. R. James Milgram, professor of mathematics at Stanford University, also a member of the Validation Committee, suggested that the CCSS contained mathematics standards that were too complex in the elementary years and not challenging enough for middle school and high school students.

The implications of any of these concerns could be catastrophic to students who will need educators to find the right balance in teaching and learning, so that concepts can be understood and properly applied. *Balance* is the operative word when discussing any learning standards that stand to influence the thinking of the majority of a given country. Many educators argue that the CCSS stifles inspiration on both the part of the teacher and the student, as increased focus is on informational text and responses that are confined to the text.

Implementing a New Curriculum

Some educators are abandoning real-life connections to learning such as inquiring about what students think about a topic and how a topic connects to a student's personal experiences. Instead, educators are focusing primarily on developing a child's ability to master evidence-based learning. Questioning in classrooms is becoming increasingly geared toward locating information within a given text. While that is a necessary exercise, asking children what they think beyond the text provides an opportunity for children to link personal experience to reading material. This can boost interest in subject areas across the curriculum.

Again, it is imperative for educational leaders to maintain balance in the implementation of best practices. As school administrators and staff study standards and curriculums, conversations around how to proceed with implementation within the context of the school culture will be necessary. Any good strategy has forethought. That stated, schools must consider potential gaps in learning that can widen if the proper measures are not taken when overhauling curriculums.

A prerequisite to those considered to be effective school leaders is finding the confidence to understand that they, along with their staff, are the experts on the unique population that makes up their student body. That is why reflective practices are so important and should be a standard practice in schools. Too many schools have become complacent—looking outside of their walls for assistance to define best practices in teaching and learning.

Educators know that if children make concrete, real-life connections to learning, they are more likely to enjoy the teaching and learning experience, and to better understand the concepts being taught. Real-life connectivity to learning needs to remain an intrinsic part of the drive to envelop students within an environment of rigor. This requires research on the part of school staff; educators should be keenly aware of students' interests.

As reflected in the CCSS, if educators want students to develop the ability to synthesize information, when a concept is initially introduced, allowing students options regarding the type of materials they read, listen to, or view is prudent. Materials aside, educators desire children to master the concept. Once they have mastered the concept, teachers can then select more complex materials for students to navigate. This requires flexibility and creativity on the part of the teacher.

Educators know that if children enjoy learning, and have opportunities to make concrete real-life connections to learning, they are more likely to have enhanced teaching and learning experiences and to better understand the concepts being taught. Educational leaders and teachers must not lose sight of this. Sometimes, the connection to learning is accomplished by linking a new concept to a child's hobbies, movie interests, favorite actors, favorite book characters, or favorite subject areas.

In the midst of the tidal wave of changes occurring in education, educational leaders should ensure that new standards are tempered with established effective practices. It is up to school leaders to encourage teachers to find innovative ways to make increased rigor accessible to children who have various learning styles and abilities. This approach supports individualized teaching and learning practices.

Assessing Students' Interests:

- In the beginning of the year, school leaders should encourage teachers to get to know their students and keep a log of students' interests. Often students approach teachers and talk about their family pet, a new baby in the home, or a hobby. Teachers listen to these stories throughout the course of a day, but rarely capitalize on them. Perhaps a child has a favorite place to visit during the summer months. If a teacher is receptive and is encouraged to jot down these tidbits, the teacher can then research materials related to the topics that most interest students, and create a catalog of materials to supplement lessons. This approach can be applied across the curriculum.

- Parents are a good source of this type of information. When school administrators and teachers have the occasion to confer with parents, being conscious of the opportunity to find out more details about a child can add value to a child's learning experiences.

- Teachers' common planning time creates an optimal setting for exchanging information about students' interest and hobbies, and how to incorporate those interests into lessons—especially for students struggling to grasp specific concepts.

- Before meeting with a student, the school and district administrators who deal directly with disciplinary issues can prepare for meetings with students by first seeking out the classroom teacher to inquire about a student's interests, both academically and socially. During conversations with students regarding discipline issues, this information can be leveraged, as it can help administrators and students form bonds, which often lead to establishing good rapport.

- A teacher once stated, "These kids don't have experiences." Every child has experiences. Not every child will take lavish vacations, but they have adventures and experiences just the same. Leaders need to ensure that there is equity in the validation of children's stories.

Educational leaders are the true lead teachers and so staff members turn to them to determine what the creative spatial boundaries will be in a given school setting. As much as possible, an educational leader should inform teachers that, within certain moral parameters, drawing on students' interests is acceptable, and should encourage teachers to do so. Getting children to a place where rigor becomes pleasurable and second nature to students is no small undertaking.

Another trend among educators worth noting is that teachers are beginning to read few to no novels in class with students, even though this was not the intention of the English language arts section of the CCSS. Much of this decline of reading full texts in class is due to the CCSS being a fairly new initiative and the focus of splitting time on content between nonfiction and informational text. The new program brings with it new teaching and learning strategies that take time for teachers to develop and master. However, thought-provoking nonfiction literature can be a viable means for critical thinking to flourish.

Introducing children to a variety of reading material has long been an effective practice in K–12 classrooms. Now, since much of the focus of the CCSS is on training teachers to teach informational text, the goal of getting children to read quality literature and diverse genres of books seems to be receding. While informational text can be beneficial to students in preparing them for college and career, fictional texts provide details that give students a well-rounded learning experience.

In colleges, professors often make reference to fictional text such as characters, famous quotes, scenes, and titles. Students who are well-rounded readers will understand these mentions. However, students who grow up in environments lacking in blended reading experiences cannot relate to such allusions. The gap created by lack of access and exposure to a variety of reading material can be addressed by educational leaders.

To avoid creating cautionary tales, school leaders must establish institutions that exemplify equity and level the playing field for all children. Not every child will be exposed to quality reading materials outside the school day. That is a stark reality.

Although many educators believe there are effective teaching and learning practices embedded in the CCSS, given the newness of the standards, school districts across the nation are closely aligning practices to the CCSS so as not to increase the chance for error when students undergo state testing that in many states are being aligned to the CCSS. However, astute educational leaders and teachers will need to make adjustments on the local level in order to truly reach the unique set of individuals they are entrusted to educate.

How can school leaders and teachers make necessary adjustments in the teaching and learning process if they fear their decisions will negatively impact test scores? This is the dilemma many school leaders and teachers face. Therefore, educational leaders are often afraid to make adjustments in the teaching and learning process that their years of experience guide them toward. It takes courage to take a calculated risk.

On one hand, the developers of the CCSS encourage states and local school districts to take ownership of the CCSS when developing state and district curriculums, but the threat of the negative impact of test results looms. This creates an atmosphere of high anxiety and low risk taking on the part of administrators. That angst is often transferred to teachers. It is therefore difficult to maintain spontaneity in instruction.

Since the stated goals of the standards are to increase rigor, where does this leave students who struggle daily with basic skill building? Many leaders are concerned about students who lack low English language arts and math skills both in the general education and special education populations. Getting these students on par often requires a variety of creative strategies.

While the majority agree that the bar needed to be raised in American educational systems, some fear that the "New Education Order" does not consider the low-performing student or those who are considered high achieving, but instead focuses on the children who fall in the midrange academically. If this is indeed the case, then this would be another major shift in education, as many parents have complained in recent decades that much of a school's special services have focused largely on the bottom-tier and top-tier students.

The alternatives that await students in our society who exit K–12 institutions with weak skills, lose interest in studies, and ultimately drop out of school, are bleak. When low-performing students do not have the proper skillsets in place to complete rigorous work, accomplishing the work becomes an impossibility. Leaders have to ensure that children complete grade 12 well equipped for life's challenges.

There is a fine line that educators walk between rigor and the impossible. When a high level of frustration and hopelessness becomes associated with learning, school and district leaders must assume a fair amount of responsibility for these circumstances. After all, they are the overseers of such breeding grounds. When desolation enters into the mindsets of students, this sets the stage for students to form disdain for the teaching and learning process.

Conversely, when educators and educational leaders ensure that students have the proper skills to accomplish demanding assignments, then with each accomplishment, self-assurance is solidified in students, and we mentally prepare students to work through complex projects. The ultimate goal is to guide students to a place where they look forward to challenges. This is a type of mental massaging that takes place between educator and student.

Just as educational leaders need to lay a foundation for change for teachers, educators must prepare students for major shifts in teaching and learning as well. The groundwork begins with basic skills. During classroom observations, it is incumbent upon administrators to help identify students' fundamental weaknesses and assist teachers in addressing core concerns.

The goal of critical thinking can only be achieved if students have the skills and confidence to master rigorous assignments. Just as every airplane requires a takeoff strip, vital measures need to be in place to ensure students can reach the heights that CCSS requires. Too often initiatives end up as slogans, not holding much meaning for parents and students. It is the school district's obligation to bring meaning to initiatives. Another initiative that often runs the risk of becoming a mere catch phrase is "College and Career Readiness."

PREPARING STUDENTS FOR COLLEGE AND CAREER

Many educational leaders have become accustomed to "slogans" such as "No Child Left Behind," "Success for All," and now "College and Career Readiness." How do school leaders and teachers bring real significance to initiatives? While college and career readiness has merit as a goal, for children who grow up without tangible, college-educated role models in their neighborhoods and households, this initiative translates into a simple slogan. Conversely, in homes and communities where college and career role models abound, the college and career readiness initiative has the possibility of being extremely effective.

School leaders can do more to massage the mindsets of students in areas of importance. In this digital age, many students respond to visual aids. In many doctors' offices one can find visual screens that loop information such as tips about staying healthy and new medications. Along the same lines, schools could use this means of "mental massaging" to introduce students to universities and trade schools from around the world. Schools only need ask alumni to submit quotes about higher learning institutions they are presently attending along with photos to post on a visual board, which would loop the information. This technique could further motivate college-bound students, and plant the proper seeds for students who are unsure of future endeavors.

Visual screens such as television or computer screens that loop information can be maintained by middle school or high school students who demonstrate interest in technology and graphic arts. The boards can be strategically placed throughout a school—in high traffic areas such as the front entrance, the cafeteria, or library. It behooves leaders to breathe life into objectives, as students need to view initiatives as being tangible.

As it concerns college and career readiness, many middle-school-age students who are surrounded by the proper role models will understand the difference between a baccalaureate degree, a master's degree, and a doctorate degree. However, these degrees can be meaningless to a student who has never been exposed to the vernacular associated with college. In many cases, educators are preparing students for a goal they know little about.

These types of oversights are not intentional on the part of educators; instead, they are the result of assumptions. Leaders and teachers rarely put themselves in the shoes of students and parents, leading many decisions in education to be determined from a slanted perspective. The parent and student reality and view can often be different from what educators assume.

While school and district leaders understand that there are tiers to accomplishing vast goals, they do not always respect the processes involved in helping students reach landings. Students can often recite the ultimate goal of their learning experiences, and college and career readiness has become a part of many schools' mission statements. However, students and parents are not always clear about what the goal will look like once it comes to fruition.

Given this, will students whom educators earnestly set out to prepare, successfully navigate college and career? Student success, K through life, has as much to do with effective communication with adults as it does a child's zip code. A child whose parent is a college graduate who does not communicate to that child the process involved in engaging in successful college and career experiences may very well be cultivating a child who is ill equipped to complete a college program or maintain a successful career.

One might believe that students can always look to their teachers and school administrators as role models. Teachers and educational leaders exemplify college and career success stories, but how many educators take the time to explain how they achieved their goals or what it takes to maintain their careers? What most children see before them each day, from their limited perspective, are ready-made products. It is imperative that the backstories of parents, teachers, and administrators be shared with students.

Remember, educational systems compete with fantasy worlds filled with unrealistic television and movie characters and virtual worlds that kids create via the Internet. Sometimes characters in their schools and neighborhoods who make "fast money" appear to be taking a viable means to a substantive career. As often as possible, teachers, school administrators, and parents should share their success journeys that were enhanced by realistic failures.

Along this vein, what is equally puzzling is that educators expect that students who have set college as a goal will successfully complete college, even though some middle- and high-school-age children cannot identify the types of undergraduate degrees that are available to them.

Similarly, parents who attempt to prevent a child from experimenting with drugs, but do not explain the potential mental and physical dangers, could be deemed irresponsible adults. These parents simply tell a child, "Don't do drugs." This alone is often ineffective in deterring children from the very danger parents want to prevent. Similarly, school officials tell children that they are preparing them for college and a career, but do little to make that vision concrete.

One effective means of making a concrete connection to college and career is by creating college and career panels of students. These panels may consist of recent alumni of the school district who are currently successfully navigating college or a career. The panel should be coordinated by school administrators, teachers, parents, and student government representatives. Ideally, the actual program should be student-led as much as possible.

These panel discussions provide a unique opportunity for middle and high school students to learn about college and career expectations directly from young adults who are not far removed in age. Often, the closeness in age between audience and speaker helps young listeners be more receptive to a given message, internalize what is being communicated, and better connect with the presenter.

The student audience can consist of a variety of clusters. For example, the panel discussion can target first-generation college-bound students or the entire student body, or panel discussions can occur simultaneously in separate rooms and target several populations of students. The panel should be blended in terms of the level of ease in which students are able to successfully navigate college and career. A realistic message for students who are on a college track to hear directly from college students is what college students would have done differently in middle school and high school in order to have made a more seamless transition to college life.

However a school decides to conduct such events, creating young college-student panels and career panels is a way of demonstrating to children that college and career are both tangible. Currently enrolled college students will be familiar faces to the school population and can offer insights to students, parents, teachers, and school administrators. There are parents who are far removed from college life and thus do not have a current perspective on obstacles that today's students face.

On the day of a college-student panel event, school administrators may opt to invite these alumni to a working lunch session with school staff to discuss how prepared those students believed they were for college, and allow alumni an opportunity to reflect on school experiences and suggest ways to improve teaching and learning. This session should be conducted in a manner that does not single out any particular staff members, but at the same time, allows young adults to speak freely.

It is one thing for students to repeatedly hear about college and career readiness from school staff, but when middle school and high school students engage with young adults who recently sat where they now sit, a third dimension is added that gives shape to life beyond K–12. The topics and questions that can be explored by staff and students are endless. Here are a few topics that middle and high school students and college-student panels can explore:

• Preparing for college

    a. Financial options

    b. Study habits

    c. What does college level work require?

    d. Building the stamina to navigate rigorous coursework

- Balancing studies and social life
- Finding appropriate support on campus

    a. Studies

    b. Psychological

    c. Financial

- Safety and health concerns relevant to college-age students
- Health insurance
- Avoiding pitfalls

    a. Time management issues

    b. Giving up when faced with challenges

    c. How/when to reach out for support

    d. Binge drinking/drugs

    e. Registering for the proper courses

    f. Prudent social media use

Giving college and career readiness a face and a voice is a component to preparedness for life beyond K–12 that students are likely to remember. Educational leaders understand that it takes multiple learning methods to reach students. Living resources breathe life into initiatives and should always be a primary consideration in implementation.

College panels give middle grade and high school students the opening to ask pertinent questions. It is prudent to incorporate a Q&A period in college-student panel discussions, as this can be extremely beneficial to educators as well as students. Both teachers and school administrators can observe the various types of college-related topics that K–12 students explore during these sessions.

Effective follow-up activities/assignments to school presentations, speakers, and panels is extremely important. The type of follow-up activities that a school chooses to conduct should be driven by the conversations students generate during these sessions. This systemic approach to K-through-life preparation will evolve as shareholders tailor these events to meet specific needs of the school or district.

SCHOOL LEADERS AND THEIR CONTRIBUTIONS TO EDUCATION

For teachers to be great, there has to exist the possibility for personal advancement, exploration of their own skills and ideas, and the prospect of taking instructional risks. Good leaders incorporate shared leadership practices into school culture. As states and school districts update curriculums around the CCSS, taking teaching styles and abilities into account will be a judicious approach to change.

In schools, it is nearly impossible for leaders to grow in a stifled environment. Many leaders, because of high-stakes testing, create their own hells. However, leaders have the choice to exercise good judgment. They first begin by defining their course of action. This is an important step, because if the leader cannot define his/her vision, then confusion among staff is likely to develop.

Systemic change can have varied definitions. A leader can interpret it as having a socialist connotation attached, wherein all parties are implementing goals in exactly the same manner. On the other hand, a leader can view systemic change as all staff within a given organization being of the same mindset and maintaining shared goals, but with varied methodologies of implementation.

The type of systemic change that provides room for individual creativity often provides opportunities for evolution to occur far beyond the original plan or expectation of the leader. This type of atmosphere is conducive to the exchange of thoughts, concepts, and original design. Conversely, very rigid systemic movement evokes fear.

When administrators give in to a heightened sense of fear, that manifests itself in an atmosphere of trepidation. Although leaders may unwittingly create such a culture, they contribute to it just the same. When teachers feel mistrust regarding school and district leaders, are not respected as experts, and are not properly supported to hone their skills, leaders fail the system and add to the poor climate that many educators complain about.

On the flip side, when educational leaders create an atmosphere of learning for teachers as well as students, then they significantly and positively impact the field of education. The professionals—school administrators and teachers—must utilize their expertise to make shifts in teaching and learning when the evidence and their experience indicate that a new direction will prove beneficial.

Being in a leadership role is a gift. Leaders have a unique opportunity to shape history, minds, and cultures. Therefore, a leader should set out to add something notable to the field of education. How can this be accomplished?

- Consistently communicate with leaders via social media—Twitter, blogs, Facebook, book clubs, and so forth.
- Maintain an open relationship with staff members so they feel comfortable sharing updates with you. That way, the leader is not the individual always initiating conversations with staff.

- Be fully present. Leaders should not become so overburdened with issues, that when staff, students, and parents are communicating them, it is evident that the leader's mind is not focused on the conversation at hand.
- Make an effort to have working knowledge of what is occurring in Professional Leaning Communities (PLCs). The leader should be up-to-date on at least the highlights. Leaders cannot effectively lead if they are unsure of in-house hot topics.
- Care. Conducive learning environments are characterized by genuine concern. There should be concern around students' and staff's health and mental well-being, a sense of responsibility regarding the life readiness of all students, and concern for the future of the country.
- Educational leaders, especially those who directly manage teachers, should maintain daily journals and write articles and books that tell about their successes and failures and what was learned from those experiences.

School and district leaders are submerged in the day-to-day occurrences in schools across the nation. These leaders are "in the moment." Yet, many do not contribute to educational publications.

A growing number are tweeting, blogging, and connected via Facebook, which is a step in the right direction. However, many of those conversations are in brief. In order to really capture and explain the more in-depth nuances of successes in education and how they were achieved, other venues such as professional journals, professional magazines, books, and quality videos would be useful.

Quality is the active word when discussing the sharing of materials between administrators, and between teachers as well. It is mind-boggling how many low-quality videos are released on You-Tube and other media outlets on a daily basis. Many administrators and teachers believe they are putting their best foot forward; creating educational videos to share with other schools and districts is a progressive idea. If the administrator has knowledge that such a video will be shared with the world, then that leader should request to view the teacher-made video that will ultimately represent the school and district. In the same token, the leader should seek the advice of fellow leaders before uploading leadership videos that will be difficult, if not impossible, to erase from the Internet world.

This does not mean that leaders should censor teacher materials. Instead, they should provide feedback that will make both the teacher and school district proud. Oftentimes, the strategies that teachers and school administrators are eager to share are great concepts, but the most important part of creating an educational video is getting the gist of the strategies across to the viewer.

The education field is certainly in need of more input from the front line. School and district leaders complain about not having enough time to read or time to develop a good piece of literature. However, both are central parts of professional learning for leaders. Retelling and sharing experiences often help a writer better understand educational processes as much as it does the reader.

There are college professors, federal and state education specialists, and educational consultants who can provide pieces of the puzzle as they relate to improving the quality of education, but the puzzle will never be complete without the firsthand accounts from school and district leaders. There are stories of failure that many school and district leaders are reluctant and embarrassed to discuss, but the lessons to be learned from those stories are valuable, as they can prevent other districts from making similar mistakes.

Find the Time to Contribute:

- Develop a cohort of school principals who share similar interests in the field. It may be easier to begin writing if all or some of these individuals agree to coauthor articles or books. These individuals can also help run a blog or a series of webinars. This makes getting your messages out to fellow administrators and teachers less taxing on any one individual leader.

- Keep a running log of events or conversations of interest that arise during the day. Using your own brand of shorthand is fine. A good way to maintain such a log is via a handheld device that is easily accessible and fits into a pocket. The material gathered can be expounded on at a later time. In addition, these notes will make for good articles, blogging, or even an informative book, given enough time.

- When a leader stumbles upon an effective method for implementing a practice, that leader can informally interview a staff member if that individual consents. Taking quick notes using a recorder throughout the day is a timesaver. There are some leaders who find this method less cumbersome than typing. This can be a convenient method, as many people have recorders built into their cellphones. Again, these notes can later be used to write and share best practices with others in the field.

- A leader should not only remain abreast of current topics, but should also think about what new elements that he/she can bring to the conversation. Publication editors seek fresh spins on current topics or divergent thinking—a school's new initiative or an entirely new approach to rolling out an initiative.

School and district leaders are the experts in educational leadership, having the most current hours on task. Other leaders in education should rightfully look to these individuals to understand the ebb and flow of teaching and learning. However, it seems that those who are deemed "experts" in the field of education are often people who are far removed from the everyday realities that school and district leaders face. Therefore, more and more, it is critical that school and district leaders find time to detail their own journeys, be willing to share both triumphs and deficiencies, and tell their stories from a collective experience given their direct dealings with parents, students, and staff.

Ideas and Questions for Getting Started

1. What topics most interest you?
2. List the hot topics in your school or district.
3. What gaps are you working to close?
4. Are there any new effective strategies that you can introduce to the field of education?
5. List some of your most memorable moments.
6. What were some of your greatest triumphs?
7. Describe your biggest challenges.
8. According to you, what elements would an ideal school possess?
9. By your standards, what qualities would highly effective teachers possess?
10. What has been your biggest administrative challenge to master?
11. What creative ways have you found to fund events, activities, building projects, supplies, and so forth?
12. How have you overcome scheduling conflicts?

13. What great leaders in history are you most like? What attributes do you share with those leaders? Which attributes of those leaders would you like to develop within yourself?

Massaging one's own mindset materializes in many ways. This list can generate meaningful conversations among fellow school and district leaders, and can act as a springboard to creating educational articles, scholarly papers, research, and other relevant literature. As administrators write and share insights, learning naturally occurs. Leaders can certainly expand this list to include other topics. The aforementioned topics will require the leader to conduct further research, hold deliberate and focused discussions with staff and other shareholders, and engage in a self-assessment exercise. Massaging the mindset for change begins with the leader's own mindset and willingness to lead transitions by example.

Many leaders have great ideas on how to move schools forward, but if they do not take the time to address the mindset, these initiatives remain dormant. Massaging the mindsets of staff is always one of the first steps in preparing for change. If done consistently, it creates an atmosphere wherein change becomes a natural part of school culture, and then leaders can spend less time addressing fragmented change issues and more time being true instructional leaders.